Northwest 3/4 West

Northwest 3/4 West

The Experiences of a Sandy Hook Pilot, 1908-1945

Captain Edward C. Winters Jr.

Edited by Mel Hardin

United New Jersey Sandy Hook Pilots' Benevolent Association
United New York Sandy Hook Pilots' Benevolent Association
Staten Island, New York
and
Mystic Seaport®, The Museum of America and the Sea®
Mystic, Connecticut
2004

Mystic Seaport
75 Greenmanville Avenue
P.O. Box 6000
Mystic, CT 06355-0990

Manufactured in the United States of America

Designed by Linda Cusano

Cataloging – in – Publication – Date

Winters, Edward C.
    Northwest 3/4 west : the experiences of a Sandy Hook pilot, 1908-1945 /
Edward C. Winters Jr. ; edited by Mel Hardin.–Staten Island, N.Y. : United New
Jersey Sandy Hook Pilots' Benevolent Association : United New York Sandy
Hook-Benevolent Association ; Mystic, Conn. : Mystic Seaport, 2004.
    p. : ill., ports. ; cm.
    Includes index.

    1. Winters, Edward C. 2. Pilots and pilotage–New York (State)–New York-
Biography. 3. Pilots and pilotage–New York (State)–New York–History–20th
century. 4. New York Harbor (N.Y. and N.J.)–Navigation–History–20th
century. I. Hardin, Mel. II. Title.
VK140.W56 A3 2004

ISBN 0-939510-89-8 (paper)
ISBN 0-939511-05-3 (cloth)

CONTENTS

Foreword

Captain Edward C. Winters, Jr. was a member of the United New York Sandy Hook Pilots' Benevolent Association, formed in 1895 as the result of legislation passed in the State of New York. Until that time, private companies of pilots licensed by either New York or New Jersey owned and operated their own pilot boats, engaging in fierce competition to pilot ships in and out of the port of New York. A long series of events eventually sparked the formation of the pilot associations. Not only had a number of catastrophic maritime accidents involving the loss of life occurred in the years leading up to "the great consolidation," but the meteorological event known as the Blizzard of 1888 also decimated the pilot boat fleet. Twelve of the seventeen pilot boats active at the time were either lost, wrecked, or severely damaged, and a number of crew and pilots were lost, making clear the vulnerability of such competitive pilot service. As a result, the legislatures of both New York and New Jersey realized that it was necessary to establish a reliable pilotage system to provide competent pilots at the entrance to the nation's largest port.

In 1895 the state-licensed pilots, who had previously worked independently and in competition with each other, were forced to consolidate their numbers into two state associations of pilots. The New York and New Jersey associations representing the licensed pilots agreed to work together, thus allowing them to pool their resources. Selling off many of their wooden sailing pilot schooners, they built a steel-hulled, steam-powered pilot boat capable of withstanding prolonged periods of adverse weather conditions. Rather than pilot schooners cruising far offshore in search of arriving ships, the new pilot boat maintained station just outside the entrance to the port to provide pilots to the ships nearing the shoals and navigational hazards. The few schooners retained by the associations continued to cruise nearby as supplemental station boats and to ferry pilots out to sea when needed. But the basic method of delivering pilots to ships, rowing them in 18-foot open wooden yawls, would remain unchanged for nearly fifty years longer.

The years following the 1895 consolidation of pilots began a long process of evolution in operational functions of the two associations. The method in which pilots agreed to work and to rotate their time on duty was refined through much trial and error. The Boards of Commissioners of each state kept a constant eye of vigilance on the associations and individual pilots, helping to shape their destiny into that which had been originally envisioned by the state legislatures. Problems involving everyday circumstances and the basic function of the Rotation Board, by which pilots were assigned to ships, were gradually solved. With the unification of the operational methods of the associations, the port's pilotage system offered highly skilled, professional pilots on a consistent basis. Vessels entering and departing the port were no longer subject to possible delay for want of a pilot, and the ever-present station boat at the entrance of the harbor gave the shipping community confidence in the reliability of the service.

Over the years I've heard and thought many times, "If

only that had been recorded for history." Maybe it was a funny account of a pilot in an unusual situation, or an experience on pilot station crowded with inbound and outbound ships, or the difficult choices presented to a pilot in the most unpleasant of circumstances that qualified as potential subjects of record. Most of these experiences are never recorded, but related from person to person until forgotten. Such is the nature of sea stories. The best survive far longer than expected, often embellished to create further interest or enhance credibility, eventually having the opposite effect. Here, however, in the transcribed text of Captain Edward Winters, are the original words and recollections of a pilot from several generations ago, set in a world quite different from ours, but with a life strangely similar to that of a modern-day Sandy Hook Pilot.

There were pilots long ago who knew that Captain Winters had written this material, but somehow it wasn't until we actively embarked on an effort to recapture the history and events concerning the Sandy Hook Pilots of the last century that these stories reappeared. Mel Hardin, hired to chronicle such history, researched many leads and stories of the pilots of the late 1800s and 1900s, and he repeatedly came across the handwritten accounts by an anonymous pilot. Finally he heard that they were written by Captain Edward Winters and eventually tracked the partial stories to Captain William "Bill" Hagen, a retired New York Sandy Hook Pilot, the stepson of Captain Winters. Bill, a well-known pilot in his own right, had the entire collection of stories in his possession and willingly shared them with Mel, who had them transcribed into print so they could be properly reviewed. More recently, Captain Hagen has generously donated them to the Associations to be preserved as part of pilot history.

Soon after the transcription it was apparent that the

entire collection, with the addition of several letters written by several pilot friends of Captain Winters, could stand alone as a book offering a pilot's-eye view of the job as he experienced it. No such book exists; indeed, the pilot's voice is usually absent from the few books about New York pilot history. As a pilot, I am struck by the conversational style Captain Winters chose to use and can relate to much of what he describes from my own experiences and my memories of numerous stories told by pilots long since retired. The depictions of his apprenticeship and life as a pilot touch chords that all of our pilots share, often with subtle humor that obviously helped him through many of his most difficult and trying experiences. It is obvious that he loved his occupation and was proud and satisfied with the work he accomplished throughout his career.

I believe Captain Winters and all of his counterparts would, given the opportunity, curiously inspect the Sandy Hook Pilot Associations of today, awed by most of the operational aspects, perhaps critical (all pilots have this innate ability) of others. For example, the very largest ships of those days are now commonplace vessels by today's standards. Ship design and propulsion improvements have changed dramatically with vastly improved hydrodynamics, building materials, specialized functions, technology integration, navigational equipment, handling characteristics, and more.

Nevertheless, the actual feel of piloting a vessel—the "touch"—remains paramount to the safe navigation of a vessel by a pilot, just as it was during Captain Winters's career. The importance of a pilot adapting to each situation aboard each vessel while compensating for the many influences—wind, seas, current temperature, visibility, precipitation, traffic, vessel draft, channel depth, crew, equipment, security, and more—remain critical to each safe transit.

The floating equipment used by the Sandy Hook Pilot Associations would be examined carefully by Captain Winters and critiqued for lines and station-keeping ability. Pilots of his era used yawls as transportation from sail- or steam-powered pilot boat to inbound vessels, rowing the open boats in all weather conditions as they were expertly launched and retrieved by the crew in close proximity to other vessels. In the years of World War II, motorized launches were introduced to accompany the station boat offshore, allowing faster transport of pilots to and from the numerous vessels in convoys leaving the port. Still, pilots of those days never trusted the wooden-hulled motorboats, sending them back to the pilot base in the event of harsh, inclement weather and opting to trust the time-proven yawls and the strength of apprentice pilots pulling the oars. Eventually, launches were built of welded steel and powered by reliable diesel engines, becoming the workhorses of the pilot service at sea, at which point the oar-powered wooden yawls became history. Not a single original example has survived.

The Sandy Hook Pilots own and operate two station boats that alternate their presence offshore at the entrance of the Port of New York/New Jersey. High-speed fully equipped aluminum launches assist the station boats to board and disembark pilots to the many commercial vessels approaching or departing pilot station. Traffic, weather conditions, and safety concerns justify the use of this particular operation to deliver pilots, and I would suspect the pilots of yesteryear would approve. However, their heads would spin if they saw some of the other options available that continue to be examined for possible future use. These options range from high-powered SWATH boats consisting of two hulls—a beam half the length of the craft—to shore-based fast delivery launches with electronic navigation stations ashore to monitor the approaches to the port. Helicopter services also exist in some ports that lower pilots aboard ships with a harness at the end of a thin stainless-steel cable unwinding from a winch, virtually eliminating the use of pilot boats most of the time.

Selection and training of pilots have changed greatly since Captain Winters's days. Competitive applications and rigorous selection methods have long replaced the practice of calling a relative or acquaintance to fill a vacancy due to the high turnover of personnel from harsh working conditions faced by an apprentice pilot. Formalized training in terms of highly monitored and overseen apprenticeships by the Pilots and Board of Commissioners of Pilots of both the States of New York and New Jersey has become standard for all pilots in training. Continued education of pilots, both junior and senior, has become necessary to help them understand and gain familiarity with the ever-changing technological upgrades of navigational equipment.

If Captain Winters were to stroll into our dispatch office, where pilots are assigned to ships as the orders are received, he would automatically look at the Rotation Board to examine the current rotation of pilots. He would inevitably grasp the basic concept of rotation, born from a system developed after the "great consolidation" of pilots in 1895 and adapted to the present-day associations. Computer monitors on office desks with databases of ships and locations, sending information instantly from the station boat and to laptop computers carried by pilots would be mystifying, of course. But despite the computers and fax machines, phone systems, cellular phones, and everything else from our world that enhances communication, it still comes down to pilots climbing aboard vessels bound in or out of the port and safely doing their jobs. He would surely nod his head in approval of the dedication and professionalism demonstrated every day by the pilots of Sandy Hook in this endeavor, carrying on a tradition that was nearly 200 years old when the United New York Sandy Hook Pilots' Benevolent Association was formed in 1895.

When Captain Winters chronicled segments of his career, the prose and narrative of earlier years took on an abbreviated form during World War II. It seems he may have struggled to keep up with his journals—the degree and frequency of piloting and the stark conditions of war making him change his writing style. His writing became more like logbook entries—short notations of events that caught his attention. Still, even in this form his entries are powerful, helping us envision the difficulty of coming to terms with the very real experiences of life and death not far from American shores. A 1947 letter from the president of the United New York Sandy Hook Pilots' Benevolent Association, Captain Edgar Anderson, reviewed activity during the war and said: "At [the port of] New York alone more than eighty thousand vessels were serviced by Sandy Hook Pilots with only two major accidents. Just imagine... when, on a particular night 254 vessels sailed or arrived at the port of New York, all serviced by Sandy Hook pilots. It has been a privilege to serve as president of this Association during one of the most interesting chapters in the history of Sandy Hook pilotage."

The termination of World War II was a turning point for the Sandy Hook Pilots. Thereafter, they focused their attention on finally addressing pilotage rates after almost fifty years so that new equipment could be obtained before their old, worn boats ceased functioning. Working conditions began to come to their attention as well, pilots slowly recovering from the sacrifice and harshness created by monstrous workloads of convoy after convoy. It was the end of an era, and an appropriate end of this particular collection of stories.

I am truly grateful to Captain Winters for his dedication to piloting and desire to record many of the situations he experienced or heard about during his career. The well-written entries provide a valuable picture of his world. We, as pilots, strongly identify with the names of pilots, jargon, working terminology, descriptions, situations, and locations he refers to in these stories. Many of us remember individuals named in the stories, and still use the same terms when discussing piloting situations—which makes it so meaningful. It is my hope that you, the reader, can also glimpse the nature of his world and job through this wonderful collection of a "gone, but not forgotten" Sandy Hook Pilot.

Captain Richard J. Schoenlank
President, United New Jersey
Sandy Hook Pilots' Benevolent
Association

Preface

On this crisp autumn night, the humidity that gives a halo effect to the thousands of lights illuminating the cables and towers of the Verrazzano Narrows Bridge was absent, and they appeared as sharp-edged as gems. In an adjacent office I could hear the usual chatter from Liz Delmar, the dispatcher, as she exchanged information with the pilot boat positioned at sea, about 20 miles from the tip of Manhattan and 12 miles from the bridge. As I continued my work of sorting through archives I heard Liz say calmly, "Yes, I can see the fire now. Is it going to be a problem?"

I could not hear the reply clearly, but the question aroused my curiosity. Then I heard Liz again, "Yes, the Coast Guard knows. Do you need assistance?"

The radio answer was garbled as I walked the few feet to the dispatchers' room window, with its unobstructed view from the tip of Manhattan down to the bridge. I looked out and could see the ship that Liz was talking with. The outbound cargo ship, 600-700 feet in overall length, was framed against the dark Brooklyn shoreline, moving steadily toward the bridge. An outward-bound ship is a common sight, but from the tall white stack of this ship a thick column of fire was shooting forth like a volcano. The calmness I heard in the dispatcher's voice as she talked with the pilot reassured me that, while this was not a usual event, it was

Rules of the Road

Meeting steamers do not dread,
when you see the lights ahead.
Green to Green, Red to Red,
perfect safety, go ahead.
*

If to starboard Red appears,
'tis your duty to keep clear.
Act as judgment says is proper
port or starboard, back or stop 'er.
*

But when upon your port is seen,
a steamer's running light of
Green, there's not so much for
you to do, for Green to port keeps
clear of you.
*

Both in danger and in doubt,
always keep a good lookout.
In danger, with no room to turn,
ease 'er, stop 'er, go astern.
*

one that was not expected to become an emergency. Liz asked, "Do you want a boat to take you off?" The answer was "No."

I watched for a few more moments as the fire shot at least 40 feet skyward from the stack. To my eye, the ship gave no indication of slowing or changing course, and very shortly it would pass directly under the bridge. The center span is 229 feet above normal mean high water, and I judged the air draft of the ship to be about 115 feet, so the bridge was not in danger. Still, having driven over the bridge hundreds of times, it amused me to think of the wonder of the drivers on the bridge, who could easily see this veritable torch approaching and might feel that they were about to drive over the flame of the world's largest Zippo lighter. But moments before the ship crossed under the span the fire went out as if an invisible hand had snuffed a candle.

This event, which has become an indelible image in my memory, seemed to cause no excitement whatsoever among the few others in the office. Within moments the Coast Guard and fireboats were all ready to assist if needed, but the marine radio didn't buzz with warnings of emergency. The cameras that monitor New York Harbor ship traffic were watching it all, and all was calm. The experience and skills of the vessel's captain and pilot were enough to make this one more quiet and uneventful night in New York Harbor.

I returned to my work of sorting through archives at the office of the New York and New Jersey Sandy Hook Pilots, who have a heritage of 310 years of guiding vessels through the complex channels of New York Bay. The ancient word pilot has been woven into many parts of our language and has, like many other words adapted, over the millennia to accept new meanings. It is has always been a word that inspires trust and implies safety—and in the ancient world the latter was in short supply. The ancient Phoenicians, who gave us the word pilot, sent out pioneering voyages around the Mediterranean world from their home port of Tyre as early as 2750 B.C.E. For them, the word meant steerer or navigator, as it still does in aviation. But at sea, for the past 300 years the word pilot has slowly changed and taken on the more specific meaning of coastwise navigator with precise local knowledge.

In June of 1999, Dr. Robert D. Ballard discovered the remains of two Phoenician trading ships in the Black Sea that sank in approximately 750 B.C.E., suggesting the range of Phoenician traders seeking new markets in those early days of navigation. Today, traders still seek new markets. But now the ship captain is responsible for the safety and overall command of the ship and cargo, while a quartermaster acts as the steerer and a navigational officer plots the course. The pilot is now a temporary visitor to the ship, boarding incoming and outward-bound vessels to direct them through the most hazardous part of their passage, in proximity to land, then departing.

Each port has a small but highly skilled group of pilots, who know the bottom configuration, the effects of wind and tide, and the complications of their port better than any ocean navigator. In the Port of New York and New Jersey, members of the New York and New Jersey Sandy Hook Pilots' Association bear responsibility to bring vessels safely in and out of what was long the nation's busiest port. Twenty-four hours a day and 365 days a year, the pilot vessel *New York* or *New Jersey* is offshore, 20 miles from the tip of Manhattan to provide pilots for ships.

Piloting is a formal business. After the pilot boards a ship and is shown to the bridge, courtesies are exchanged between the captain of the vessel and the pilot. The captain then gives the pilot permission to take charge of the helm and give continuous navigational directions to the quartermaster who steers the ship. These directions are in the form of specific compass points to follow, which have to take into account the direction and strength of the wind, the state of the tide, and the draft of the vessel, as well as any known shifts in the fickle sand channels leading into the port. These channels may shift slightly and vary with every tide and storm. If wending a long and not very responsive vessel through the maze of channels, the tangle of harbor traffic, and the confinement of bridges were not enough, it is the pilot's task to know how the vagaries of nature can affect the navigation of individual ships everyday.

All foreign-flag vessels and American vessels under register are required by state law to take on a pilot to navigate in the port. Because of the skills and knowledge required in each port, pilots are welcomed to take the helm, guaranteeing the safety of millions of dollars of cargo. A ship that slips off course and runs aground can block a channel, interrupting the delicately timed and balanced flow of commerce, or, if carrying the volatile cargoes that travel by sea, can threaten the harbor environment and the safety of port residents.

A formal system of licensed pilots was created by the New York Legislature in 1694 to guarantee pilotage for His Majesty's ships and to assure their safe passage in and out of the Port of New York. Although the port was busy in 1694, only two men were named as pilots. They were required to live in the harsh and remote environment of the barrier sandspit called Sandy Hook, and they rowed to and boarded ships in Sandy Hook Bay, New Jersey. This was the origin of what the maritime world now knows as the Sandy Hook Pilots.

In the association's small modern building on the north

shore of Staten Island, I had spent almost one year going though yellowed newspapers and file folders filled with brittle documents. Many shattered pages had to be reconstructed just to read the words, which were in many cases not relevant to my search. But I turned every page and read every fragment, trying to update a history that was last told in Edward Russell's *From Sandy Hook to 62 Degrees*, published in 1929. The files I was reading covered the period from about 1870 to 1960. Having read Russell's book, it was obvious to me that he had never seen these materials. From my fluorescent-lit perspective I realized that I was the first person who had full access to this private maritime history, much of which was recorded by gaslight or kerosene lamp.

The pilots kindly volunteered an office for me to use as a collection center for the many boxes of accumulated historical materials, and more would appear without warning. I finally protested, saying, "This is a modern and small building, not a 56-room Victorian house with hidden rooms. Where is the source of all this material?"

New Jersey President Richard Schoenlank would grin and say, "Well, I just found this box and thought you would be interested in these papers." Feigning pain, I was nonetheless always happy when more material was found.

Most of the material dated after the 1874 introduction of the commercial typewriter and what we consider to be the birth of the modern office. Because of the exponential growth of American business, massive ledgers gave way to file folders to hold business communications in the early 1900s. Sometimes hundreds of business-related newspaper clippings were pasted into large albums. Today everything would be placed on thin plastic diskettes in electronic form and perhaps deleted after a designated time.

While many of the files I went through were about the business of piloting, I could see that the hands of many people had clipped the stories about ship collisions, a fight between the fireboat and a salvage boat over who was entitled to put out a fire, an 1890 story about a brief pilot mutiny, the many clippings of the first America's Cup yacht race (yes, there was a Sandy Hook pilot at the helm of the yacht *America* in 1851, when she won the Hundred Guinea Cup that became the America's Cup), and engraved newspaper images of every ship in Admiral Sampson's 1898 fleet. The boxes contained the letters to and from steamship companies, a note from the King of Sweden apologizing for a collision between a Swedish ship and a pilot boat, a letter of praise from President Roosevelt, and letters from World War II, when the pilots feared the U.S. Navy takeover of all pilotage in New York Harbor meant they would lose their vessels and jobs forever. All of the papers were interspersed with obituaries and reports of tragic pilot accidents.

After more than six months of reading, repairing, treating paper for acidity, copying, and filing, I came across a handwritten story in a box of loose and unfiled material. It was a second- or third-generation photocopy of a story titled "The Blizzard of 1888." The script was faint, but with patience I could decipher most of the words. It was a firsthand account of one of the most catastrophic storms in New York City history. The infamous "White Hurricane" was responsible for over 400 deaths and the loss or wrecking of twelve pilot schooners. The pilot boats *Enchantress* and *Phantom* were lost with all hands on board. The writer identified himself as the son of the boat keeper on the pilot boat *Pet* #9, who had experienced the storm. Of all of the papers I had seen thus far, this was first handwritten account that I suspected was composed by a pilot.

In the next few weeks I found two more photocopies of handwritten stories. It was easy to recognize the handwriting and style as being by the same man, but there was no clue to his identity. I asked some of the older pilots who passed through the office as they came and went from ships. They agreed that the stories gave a great picture of piloting, but they had no idea who had written them.

The next summer the pilots association encouraged me to interview retired pilots in Florida. I drove the entire Florida coastline interviewing senior pilots, several of whom began their service before World War II. I had a very strong feeling that the person who had written the stories would have been a senior pilot when the men I was interviewing were apprentices, and I hoped they would have known him. During World War II, with huge ship convoys moving in and out of New York, as many as 125 pilots worked in the Port of New York. However, the pace of the work then was such that many pilots knew those they had apprenticed with, but they didn't know senior pilots very well. Several said they had heard that a pilot was writing about pilot history, but they couldn't identify him.

After returning to New York, I found several copies of letters from Pilot Ed Ronayne, written in the same handwriting and on the same lined paper as the mysterious stories. Thinking I had a lead, I searched New York City records for surviving members of the Ronayne family, but could find none.

For several months I had been encouraged to meet the Huus brothers, two retired pilots about whom many pilots had spoken with great affection and respect. I arranged to interview Carl and William Huus in Camden, Maine. Carl Huus lived in Camden and William (Bill) Huus had volunteered to drive over from Lake George, where he was the captain of a sidewheel excursion boat. Both brothers were in their eighties. At some moment during the visit I showed them a copy of the stories. By then, asking the author's identity had become a part of the interview process, and as usual I was prepared for another negative response. To my utter and profound astonishment, Bill Huus said, "Sure, Ed Winters wrote this story and many more." He then asked if I would like a copy of the complete set.

A week or so later the mail brought a thick envelope containing faint copies of more than a hundred handwritten pages. All were done on the same lined paper, in the same handwriting, and written on a few was the name Ed Winters.

Finally I had the author's name. I went again to the pilots in the New York Office to find the official records of Edward Winters and to check if he had a family who might still have the original copies of the stories. I hoped they might permit them to be published, for I considered them to be a treasure of maritime history.

Ed Winters was a second-generation pilot born on Staten Island. A pilot having a son follow him in the business isn't unusual, and a few families can count five generations in piloting. Many pilots said that they had heard the name, but evidently Ed Winters didn't have a son who became a pilot. I couldn't find any Winters family, but on Staten Island the name Winter with no "s" is a very old family name. I was told by members of the Winter family that they thought the Winters line had died off. Once again, it appeared that I was at a total dead end.

One fall evening at least two months later I was in the pilot office when Captain Howard Hill came in from sea. I had known Captain Hill (now retired) since 1984 and remembered that his family was also from Staten Island. I asked, "Howard, please help me with this mystery. I think Ed Winters is the one who wrote these stories. Why can't I find any relatives of Edward Winters?"

After two years of searching, this one serendipitous

encounter with Howard Hill filled the void. Captain Hill replied, "I knew Ed Winters; both his and my families were from Great Kills, Staten Island." He continued: "Ed Winters was a retired pilot when I was a 20-year-old young apprentice. Captain Winters had adopted two children, a brother and sister. The son also became a pilot. His name is Bill Hagen, and he is very much alive and has retired and lives in New Jersey."

With ease I found his telephone number, and when I called I was greeted by a very friendly Captain William Hagen, who confirmed that Ed Winters was his stepfather. I told him that I had found a few stories that I thought had been written by Ed Winters and was curious if he wrote more. Captain Hagen responded brightly, "Yes, he did. In fact, I have the entire notebook of all of his stories."

Within a few days I drove the 60 miles to visit Captain Hagen and his wife, Esther. Captain Hagen took me outside to show me his pond. As we approached, fish began to swim to the edge. "They know me 'cause I feed them," Captain Hagen said and, with obvious joy, he tossed a small handful of grain into the churning waters. After a few moments of enjoying the fish, we headed back to his kitchen.

William G. Hagen, was a very young 78 when we spoke. He recalled that Ed Winters graciously sponsored him to become a pilot. He began his apprenticeship in 1942 and became a pilot on January 29, 1950. He retired in 1989. "Whenever I think of Ed, past or present, it's always a plus. He was a very kind and understanding man who would listen intently before giving you a reply. As a pilot and fellow shipmate, Ed had an aura that commanded respect, a quality I shall always remember. I always wished I had Ed's talent for writing, but then again, he was a lousy golfer."

Then, Captain Hagen handed me an old loose-leaf

binder. For the first time, I saw the complete set of hand-written stories, all on numbered pages. They were all clear, written by a confident man who never lined out a word in revision. I thumbed through quickly and found what I was looking for. Seeing a smile on my face, Bill asked, "What did you find?"

"It's here," I said. "The Blizzard of 1888. This is the first story I found, over two years ago." Even though the storm occurred five years before Ed Winters was born, there can be little doubt that he heard the details from his father, Edward C. Winters Sr. (1861-1946), who was boat keeper of the pilot schooner *Pet* #9 during the storm.

Captain Hagen then offered me full access to the writings of his stepfather. More recently, he has generously donated the writings to the New York and New Jersey Sandy Hook Pilots Association so they will be preserved, as well as published in this form.

To top it all off, he even had Ed Winters's photo album, which he had assembled as meticulously as he had composed his stories. Many of the photographs in this book are from that album, offering a rare depiction of the men and boats who figure in these stories.

I asked Captain Hagen to contribute some of his memories of being an apprentice, and he offered the following, which reinforce his stepfather's written accounts of the ways young apprentices blew off steam as they learned a hazardous and demanding job.

"As apprentices we were always competing between the inside boat and the outside boat. We would have yawl races out on station, rowing from the sea buoy to the entrance buoys of Ambrose Channel and back, a distance of over four miles. With a northwest wind and ebb tide it was a struggle inbound, but back to the sea buoy was a snap with fair tide and wind. We took a lot of pride in our yawlmanship, especially when we won, or rowing in an easterly gale.

"Life on the outside boat was never dull. We were always playing pranks on each other, like carefully tying a sleeping shipmate to his bunk and then placing three or four live lobsters on his body and awakening him. Apprentices were always on call and kept their shoes ready at the side of the bunk. It was not uncommon to wake up and find your shoes screwed to the deck so that, when you sleepily slipped your feet in them on, you fell forward on your face. A stray bucket of cold water coming from nowhere was common.

"During an extended period while we were tied up on the inside boat, we had a model apprentice who was a bit paranoid about things missing from his locker. These wooden lockers were roughly 20 inches by 20 inches by 36 inches deep. To thwart any intruders, our friend installed a metal hasp and a combination lock. He overlooked one item—the outside hinges had removable pins. Shortly before he returned to the boat from his time off, we removed the door and installed a wild cat that we caught from the pier. This cat was really mad! The model apprentice comes aboard and goes directly to his eye-level locker to stow his gear, dials the secret number, opens door, and out flies the screaming cat all over our friend.

"There was a time when silverware, soap, and towels were disappearing from the outside boat. To stymie this crime, all apprentices' bags were searched before going ashore. This was a perfect setup for the bad boys athletic club. The checkpoint was on deck, just before the pilot and apprentice got into the motorboat to board a ship. Somehow—thanks to the bad boys—some of these items were found in model apprentice's bag. This inspection was done by the boat's captain and in the presence of a pilot, both of whom were in on our caper. Tears rolled down the cheeks of model apprentice, who was of course in complete denial. After a severe reprimand he was allowed to go ashore."

Like Bill Hagen's memories, Edward Winters's stories reveal much of the playfulness of these serious men. For the reader's ease, the individual stories, which were written down as he thought of them, have been arranged in chronological order and organized into chapters. The concluding story that describes his accident is quoted from his report to the pilot Board of Commissioners. The text has been lightly edited throughout, and vessel names have been corrected where necessary and possible. Reminiscences of several of Winters's fellow pilots, which he collected, have been included in the appendix. As noted, many of the illustrations are drawn from an album kept by Edward Winters, which was in possession of Bill Hagen. Others are from the collections of the Sandy Hook Pilots' Association, and still others, so marked, are in the collections of Mystic Seaport.

For their assistance in bringing this work to completion, I wish to thank the following individuals and institutions: Captain Howard R. Hill, Sandy Hook Pilot (ret.), for his interest in pilot history that launched this project; Captain William and Esther Hagen for allowing me complete access to the documents and photos and for answering my many questions; Captain Richard J. Schoenlank, President of the United New Jersey Sandy Hook Pilots' Benevolent Association; Captain William W. Sherwood, President of the United New York Sandy Hook Pilots' Benevolent Association; Captain Leo Kraszeski, Merchant Mariner (ret.), Sailors' Snug Harbor Foundation; the members of the United New York and New Jersey Sandy Hook Pilots' Benevolent Associations, both active and retired, who patiently answered my many questions; Sharon Nee for her accurate transcriptions of Edward Winters's stories; the New York Public Library Rare Books and Microfilm Libraries; the staff of the G.W. Blunt White Library at Mystic Seaport; Andrew German, Director of Publications at Mystic Seaport; and my wife Peg and daughter Jessica, who patiently did without a dining room table for more than a year as I pieced this story together.

Mel Hardin
Staten Island, New York

Mel Hardin has written for *Sea History Magazine* and co-authored an article about Herman Melville for Melville Society Extracts. He has been Historic Site Director of Snug Harbor Cultural Center-Staten Island, where he designed and created maritime history exhibits that have won awards from the New York State Council on the Arts. Currently he is Curator/Conservator of the Maritime Collection of Sailors' Snug Harbor Foundation in North Carolina.

Captain Edward Carsten Winters Jr.

Edward Carsten Winters Jr. was born on May 21, 1893, in Tompkinsville, New York, the Staten Island community overlooking New York Bay where many of the harbor pilots lived. Following his father's lead, he entered the New York Sandy Hook Pilot service on August 6, 1908, at the age of 15, serving as crew on the steam pilot boat *New Jersey*. He became registered as a New York apprentice on May 23, 1911, and then registered as boat keeper exactly two years later. During this time he served on the sailing pilot schooners *Ambrose Snow* #2 and *Washington* #5. On May 16, 1916, he was granted his original state license as a pilot, limited to vessels with a draft of not more than 18 feet. One year later his draft limitation was lifted to 24 feet, and a year following that it became 28 feet. One year after that, in 1919, he became a full branch pilot, qualified to navigate the many channels of the port. Old records indicate that in 1931 his license was unlimited in draft and tonnage, and entry confirmed that he remained a pilot of the 1st grade–Full Branch.

He continued piloting until he injured his back in late December of 1945, when a Jacob's ladder broke as he climbed the side of an American tanker at sea. Apprentice Pilot Bill Hagen, his stepson, happened to be rowing the yawl at the time. He recalled that Captain Winters suddenly came crashing down and landed in a sitting position on the gunwale of the yawl. He then fell into the sea, only to be hauled aboard the yawl by two apprentices, one of them being a desperate Bill Hagen—then a 160-pound young man struggling with a 250-pound pilot. Captain Winters was on the sick list from January 1 to April 15, 1946. He returned to piloting until November 13, 1947, when he went on the sick list again, eventually retiring from the Sandy Hook Pilots on December 5, 1948.

During his final years as a pilot he was instrumental in starting a more structured educational program for apprentice pilots to learn the craft of piloting in the Port of New York/New Jersey. He drafted a number of written lessons that each apprentice was expected to complete in preparation for licensing examinations.

After retirement, Captain Winters eventually moved from Staten Island, New York, to Canadensis, Pennsylvania, where he and his wife Marian lived in a white clapboard house perched atop a hill, far from the sea. There he lived comfortably for many years, walking daily with his cherished Samoyed dog, Lux, and sitting on the front porch smoking his pipe and reading. He never accepted the prospect of flying anywhere, but liked the idea of taking the train to other places. He traveled occasionally to Chicago and elsewhere during his retirement, and kept in touch with active and retired pilots alike, including his cousin Phil Winters.

Edward C. Winters Jr. lived until February 4, 1975, succumbing at the age of 81.

Following on page xxx
Pilot Chart of the Channels and
Courses of New York Bay, 1926
(Courtesy Howard Hill)

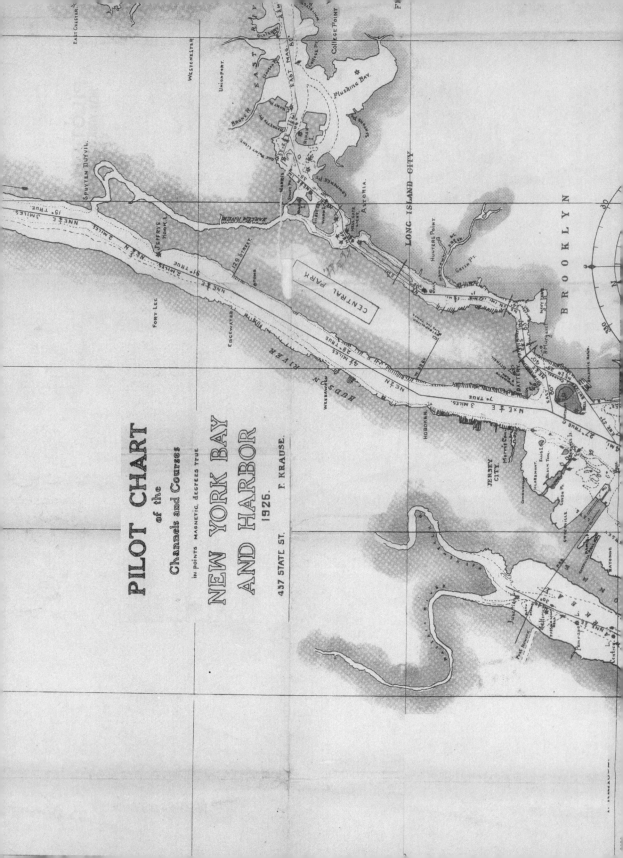

PILOT CHART

of the
Channels and Courses

in POINTS MAGNETIC, DEGREES TRUE

NEW YORK BAY
AND HARBOR
1926.

F. KRAUSE.
457 STATE ST.

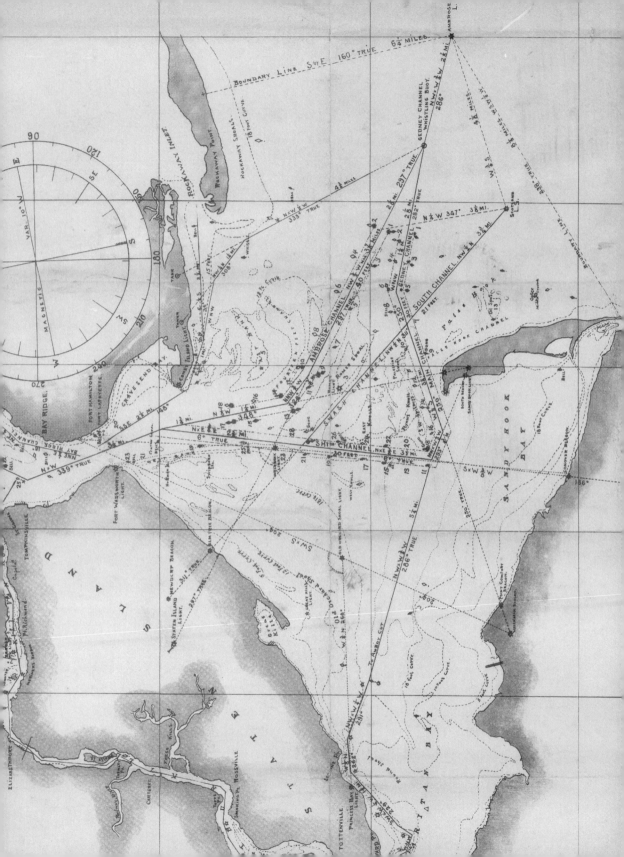

Chapter One

"S-S-S-Sou'west, Sir"
Learning to Be a Pilot under Sail, 1908-1916

My dad was born in Osterholz, Sharmbek, Germany, April 16, 1861. He came to the U.S. quite young and shipped in a small two-masted schooner, *Chincoteague*, coasting between New York and the James River, Virginia, carrying oysters, sweet potatoes, and sometimes poultry and sheep. On numerous occasions she ran into a harbor similarly named. He also sailed on the square-riggers *Columbus*, *Virginia*, and *Seminole*, "rounding the Horn" once.

He served his time on pilot boat *Pet* #9, being boat keeper during the Blizzard of 1888. He received his license October 22, 1889 and became part owner of the *James Stafford* #18, which replaced the *Enchantress #18* lost during the blizzard, March 13, 1888.[1] His partners in *#18* were Oscar Stoffreiden, Joe Nelson, Gus Peterson, Martin Reierson, and Elvin Mitchell. She was lost on the Romer Shoal, Gabe Conney, boat keeper.[2]

In the early 1900s the British tanker *Iroquois* (draft loaded to 29 feet), commanded by Captain Scott, would tow the six-masted barge *Navahoe* (draft loaded at 30 feet, 6 inches) across to England loaded with gasoline. The tow was made up off Stapleton on the flood tide and used the Main Ship Channel. One time my dad was pilot of the *Iroquois* and started to sea late on the tide, with poor visi-

[1] The blizzard of March 11-14, 1888, sometimes called the Great White Hurricane, was responsible for more than 400 deaths and the loss or wrecking of 12 pilot schooners. The pilot boats *Enchantress* and *Phantom* were lost with all hands.

[2] In 1894 the Sandy Hook Pilots consisted of New York Pilots who owned 20 boats and had 130 pilots, and the New Jersey Pilots who owned eight boats and had 56 pilots. "Each pilot boat is owned by a company of five to seven men who own shares in the schooner which is usually 50 to 80 tons. Besides the pilots the boat carries a crew composed of four seamen, a cook who is the most important person on board, and a boat keeper. The latter takes charge of the boat and takes her home after the last pilot has gone aboard a vessel." Once a Week, November 29, 1894.

Pilot Edward C. Winters Sr. poses with his son (the author) and daughter Tillie, ca. 1910. (Courtesy William G. Hagan)

bility. They got the ebb tide and dense fog below the Narrows, but towing the barge on a short five-inch wire hawser he couldn't stop—they had to keep going. He took a chance and towed down Ambrose Channel (barred to tows without special permission) with fog so thick he couldn't see the barge astern, made the turns safely, and luckily avoided all the vessels anchored outside on a strong following tide. Good piloting, but what a thrill!

Sometime in the 1920s, the *Berengaria* (ex-Majestic) sailed from Pier 54, North River, Captain Irwin in command with my dad as pilot. They had fog all the way down the Bay, and outside it was dense with a fresh southerly breeze. Dad felt his way between anchored ships, looking and listening for the pilot boat. The skipper became anxious with bells of anchored vessels all around. He asked my dad to take him clear, outside the lightship. My father did, and after further delay the skipper said, "Pilot what do you say about the trip to England. We'll make you comfortable; can't wait for the pilot boat any longer." My dad said, "OK," and away they sailed. They arrived in England five days later, and he boarded the White Star steamship *Alban* (ex-*Bismarck*), sailing for New York. This turned out to be a nice 11-day vacation, which cost the Cunard Line $3.00 per day detention for the pilot.[3]

He retired April 16, 1931, his last ship being the "Para" boat *Hermit* in with a load of rubber from Brazil. He died at 1:10 A.M., January 1, 1946. His father, Herman, was born in 1827.

It was on a night in November 1906 that New Jersey pilot boat *Hermit* #7 was maneuvering to board the Ward Line (New York & Cuba Mail Steamship Company) steamship *Monterey*. The ship was getting dangerously close when my cousin, Phil Winters, was ordered to burn a torch to indicate the pilot boat's position and heading. The *Monterey* struck the *Hermit* with some force, knocking Phil, torch, and all overboard. She started to sink at once, and the men managed to get away in a yawl. Phil was floundering around in the dark with the yawl looking for him. He was finally going down from exhaustion when John McCarthy looked over the side and grabbed Phil by the hair, rescuing him. It was a close shave for Phil, but Frank Neilson of the same crew later died of injuries. All hands were saved, but the *Hermit* left her bones south of Scotland Lightship.

[3] On occasion, usually due to extreme weather conditions, a pilot may not be able to leave the ship he is piloting out of the bay and must accompany it to its next port. This is called being "carried off." In picking up or discharging a pilot, a ship is required to "make a lee" to shelter the small pilot yawl while it is alongside. For the large, strictly scheduled passenger liners, it might take too long to make a lee in gale winds and seas to await the yawl, so it was not uncommon for a pilot to have a nice cruise to Southampton, England, as the guest of the shipping company.

The pilot schooner *Hermit* #7 in light airs under full sail: her "four lowers"—mainsail, foresail, forestaysail, and jib—plus a flying jib, a fisherman staysail between the masts, and a main topsail above the mainsail. For winter work in heavy winds, the mainsail carries three bands of reef points and the foresail two bands to shorten them down. The forestaysail has a "bonnet" (removable section) laced to the foot—the lacing making a dark horizontal band—and a set of reef points as well. The 80-foot *Hermit* was built as the *James G. Bennett* #7 at Brooklyn in 1893. Her number remained the same, though she was renamed. She was sunk by the steamship *Monterey* in November 1906. (Courtesy William G. Hagen)

On December 14, 1907, pilot Thomas Shields had the Norwegian steamship *Talisman* to sea. There was a southeast gale, heavy sea and snow when the pilot boat New York dropped her yawl to take him out. Phil and Billy Canvin got alongside the ship, took Mr. Shields off, and started back to the New York. A huge sea struck the yawl, capsizing it and throwing all three into the water. After awhile the New York came alongside the men, throwing lines to them. Phil and Billy were hauled aboard, but Mr. Shields, exhausted, drowned. The two boys were given a week off to recover, without pay. Things were tough in those days. Mr. Al Beebe was "super" (marine superintendent).

It was August 2, 1908; the day was sunny and the wind was south. The pilot boat *New Jersey* was storing up at Brady's (Long Dock) at the foot of Prospect Street, Staten Island, where I joined her. I had turned fifteen in May and was a tall skinny kid just out of 2B, Curtis High School. Jack Lyle (Turps) was captain, Tom Port was mate, Carl Huus was boat keeper, Lewis was chief engineer. I was initiated into the forecastle by the deck crew: Arthur Peterson, Willie (Fuppe) Mitchell, Frank (Nosey) Peterson, Ernest Sloat, and Johnny Hauffman—all good shipmates.

We used to store up weekly at Brady's Dock, also called Long Dock, at the foot of Prospect Street. There was a grain elevator on the south side inner end and a square wooden

In this view toward the Narrows from Staten Island, ca. 1905, Bechtel's Basin and the Long Dock on the Stapleton waterfront lie at the center of the photo. The pilot schooner *Washington* #5 lies off the Long Dock with mainsail raised as oceangoing ships pass up and down the bay, each requiring a pilot on board. (Mystic Seaport, 1985.74.6)

Chapter One

Disabled Steamer

If a vessel disabled and
cannot well steer,
By breakdown of engines or
perhaps steering gear.
Two lights she will show
from her fore-mast head,
One under the other and
both of them red.
By day two balls hoisted in
this same position,
Will explain to all vessels
her helpless position.

shed near the outer end. Dead horses were deposited there for collection by the Department of Health, using their dead-horse covered wagons drawn by two horses. These dead horses were picked up by the "dead horse boat," the *Islander*, a steam lighter which could carry 10 or 12 on her foredeck. These she took to Barren Island, Jamaica Bay, for rendering and disposal. On store days our boats would tie up about 15 or 20 feet from this shed and in the summer they would be filled with flies in no time. We had no "Flit guns" in those days but used 8x12 inch sheets of "Tanglefoot" sticky fly paper, poison paper, and fly cages baited with little Hannes Eilman's good lager beer. The Ocean Yacht Club lay just south of the Long Dock at the foot of Water Street. The "New Dock," later Pier 14, was built about 1910, and a large four-masted, twin-screw, French freighter, *La Pérouse*, 30-foot draft, used to dock there. Just below this was Jaburgs and then the Staten Island Yacht Club. Below this was Merritt, Chapman's salvage yard, then the Baltimore & Ohio railroad yard. One of our older boys, Frank Miller, built a float and ladder at the Staten Island Yacht Club for the pilots' use. We also used the float at the New Dock, corner of Water and Bay. The Michael sisters, Daisy and Minnie, had a candy and soda store on the northeast corner(later bought by Whelan). Bill Gould, who had a Whitehall boat and made a living rowing men to and from ships, was rumored to have more lives than a cat, falling overboard numerous times as a result of too much Peruna, finally "took the veil," as the saying goes. On his good behavior he went to Michael's, had a soda, and when leaving the store he fell and broke his leg. He immediately swore off sodas and went back to something safer. Rita Farley sold tickets at the Staten Island Rapid Transit (SIRT) station at Stapleton (a fine girl) and later married Pilot Arthur Peterson. Charles P. Hoefer, agent for Dr.

Brown's Celery Tonic, also a seltzer-water bottler, lived on Prospect Street near Richmond Road.[4]

The old German Club Rooms owned by Troebners, Steinbacks and later Viemersters, were on the northwest corner. Horrmans lived on this street; their property running through to Beach Street. Badenhousens lived with them. Pilots Al Beebe, Walter Brinkman, Frank Beebe, and Phil Winters lived on Beach Street; also Arthur Thompson, lumber dealer, Louie Birkel, soft drinks, Professor Crane and son, Loyal Mike Cahill, Johnny Howarth, Dr. Vidal, Reve Max Krueger, and Mr. Broughton, a nice old British artist for whom I posed for a quarter a throw. Baer, the photographer, and daughter, Phillipina. Fred Spouse lived where the Liberty Theater later stood. The Police Station, Bardes the butcher, Feldhusen and Arthur Wilshaw also were on the street. Beissman's, later Herman's, had a store at the corner of Beach and Richmond Road. John Siemer on the southwest corner, Dr. Ware, Lucy, Goodwin, Burkhardts, later Farrs all on Richmond Road. Kuhnemund's store corner of Wright Street, Hugo Traege's music shop, Ilma Wolf, Kuscheraks, Rosenbergs, Effie Cocksehutt, Louie Schwarz lived on Wright Street.

North of the Long Dock, at the foot of Wave Street, was the "Penny Dock," where George Stapleton tied up his little waterboat *Scandinavia*, and later the *George W. Stapleton*. He supplied our sailboats with water, and, when the ice started running heavy during the winter, would tow them to Mariner's Harbor for lay-up. The "Dog Pound" ASPCA was located on Wave Street alongside the SIRT. Bechtel's Basin was an L-shaped dock at the foot of Elizabeth Street that served as a landing for Coney Island boats and the side-wheeler *Mt. Desert*, a fishing boat. Some sail pilot boats tied up inside the L, as did the yacht *Karina* and the square-rigger *Jacob A. Stamler*. There was an icehouse on the bulk-

[4] The present Staten Island office of the Sandy Hook Pilots is across the street from the old Ocean Yacht Club.

Chapter One

Safe Piloting at Night

*When both side lights you
    see ahead,*
*Port your helm and show
    your red,*
Green to green, red to red,
Perfect safety, go ahead.

If on the Port tack you steer,
It is your duty to keep clear.
*Of every close hauled ship
    ahead,*
*No matter whether green or
    red.*

*But when upon your port is
    seen,*
*A stranger's starboard light
    of green,*
There's not so much for you to do,
*For green to port keep clear
    of you.*
Both in safety and in doubt,
Always keep a good lookout.

head, and a floating bath was moored on the north side during the summer. Dan Britton was in charge, and I learned to swim there. Thompson's Lumber Yard joined it on the south and west. Pat O'Brien had his horseshoe shop between SIRT and Bay Street. Just north of the L Dock ran a breakwater, which sheltered motorboats and where we also swam. The SIRT ran north and south into the "Killey Pond," where Pete Murphy had his boatyard. As boys, we used to get a thrill by standing on this trestle until a train approached. Then we would drop down between the ties and hang on, suspended, while the train passed over us. I did this once too often, when some hot ashes from the firebox dropped on my neck, which gave me a good burn that I had difficulty explaining away when I got home. Just north was the I.T. Williams Lumber Yard and log basin, at the foot of Clinton Street. North of this was Martineau's Dock, then the American Docks, with a naval landing on the south side. The revenue cutter *Mohawk*, and later the *Seneca* ("Cardigan's Mad House") sat off these piers. After World War I, Mayor Hylan had new Piers 7 to 21 built. Up the street from American Docks were the Baltimore Flats, and George L. Egbert (Egbert the hatter) had a men's shop and sold the popular "Pilot's Caps," made out of heavy blue cloth, for 75 cents. Oswald and Tichenor had a similar store in Stapleton.

Storing up a sailboat was work and consisted of a barrel of flour, a quarter ton of ice, a quarter ton of coal, a large basket of meat, plus vegetables and dry stores, all of which had to be loaded into a yawl at Brady's and then rowed off to the boat anchored below Pier 14. This generally took two trips, but one of my shipmates tried to do it all in one trip, alone, by sculling. He started off loaded to the gunwales and was swamped by the swells of a passing B&O tug, sinking the yawl, which was never seen gain. We saw this from the boat and saved his life with another yawl, as he couldn't swim.

Storing the steam pilot boats *New Jersey* or *New York* generally took place after coaling up at Port Johnson, New Jersey, on the Kills. It consisted of taking aboard about one and one half tons of ice from Brady's, lowered in cakes through the hatch in the crew's mess room to the iceboxes in the hold. There was also coal for the galley from Brady's. Our meat was delivered by Bardes, Horn Lambert depending upon who was super. Bruns of East India Tea Company delivered the dry stores; Carstensen, Lippman, Messino the fruits and vegetables. Frank Weber, Louie Mueller, Addie Pape were ship chandlers and handled hardware. Granata was the popular package liquor dealer. Anton Stuhl, Hanne Eilmann, Emil Tiedes, Joe Rapp, Troebner's German Club Room, Kingsingers, Lena Guenthers, Paul Stolpes were popular thirst-slacking emporiums. The Grain Factory was located just west of Stapleton Station of the SIRT, and Brady's Ice and Coal was just east of the same station. Old man Brady had white whiskers and a fine daughter, Genevieve, who later married Charlie McAteer. In the office were Miss Martin and Miss Hess (Mrs. Richter). Pilots kept their seabags in a special room adjoining, and we boys lugged them to the boats for the pilots bound to sea.

At this time there was a "Station Company" of five men, who spent one week on the *New York* on Inside Bar Station, then returned, boarding no ships except those that got by the outside boats. "Doggie" Kelsey was captain of the *New York*, a short 5x5, kindly man. Johnny Swainson was mate. The *New Jersey* held Eastern Station; the *New York* held Bar Station; and the sailboats *Ambrose Snow* #2, *Washington* #5, and *Trenton* #4 (ex-*Kernwood*, which in 1907 replaced the sunken *Hermit* #7) rotated on Southern Station with six pilots apiece.[5]

[5] The *Kernwood* was a fishing schooner built in 1904.

Chapter One

The *New Jersey* (#3), built at Tottenville, Staten Island, in 1902, is seen here underway on the pilot grounds. The 157-foot, single-screw, wooden-hulled vessel was also suitable for ice-breaking in winter. She remained in service until the steamship *Manchioneal* collided with and sank her in July 1914. Built for seakeeping, the *New Jersey* has a sheltering whale-back deck forward. Two lifeboats are on davits amidships. The pilot yawls are on deck, one on each side, beneath the hoisting booms on the mainmast. Note the pilot flag at the main truck. (Courtesy William G. Hagen)

In the office take-off time was 9:45 A.M. and 4:45 P.M. The New Jersey office was on the fourth floor, the New York office on the eighth floor of 17 State Street. Bart Stump, Dave Little, and Jim Melville ran the New Jersey office.

New York's first steam-powered pilot boat, the *New York* (#1) was known as the "Trolley" because she made regular trips up and down the bay to deliver pilots. Here she steams out through the Narrows. The 155-foot, single-screw, steel-hulled *New York* was built at Wilmington, Delaware, in 1897 and remained in service until 1951. By the time this photo was taken she had been equipped with wireless communications. (Courtesy William G. Hagen)

The 82-foot pilot schooner *Ambrose Snow #2* was built at Brooklyn in 1888 as #12 and was renumbered in the late 1890s. (Courtesy William G. Hagen)

Morris Riker, George Gaa, and John Pillion ran the New York office. Mr. Nash and the late Captain Appelby were New York Commissioners. The secretary, his daughter, who held a sail license, did typing and later married Pilot Tom Port.

In 1908 each office had its own board, and the men were apportioned on a seven New York/three New Jersey basis for the Sea Company. On the Board was an Inward and an Outward. The men on the Outward were assigned to vessels as they cleared and were responsible for them until then sailed. Pilot Johnny Kiernan once was assigned to a schooner on clearance and remained "on" that vessel until she sailed weeks later. She was held up by unfavorable winds and weather, and a skipper who was having a good time ashore.[6]

6 Winters means that after the merger of the New York and New Jersey pilots, on any day the ratio of pilots working was 70 percent New York pilots, 30 percent New Jersey pilots. As is the case today, the pilots were listed on a large rotation board on the wall, which was divided into inward- and outward-bound columns, and their assignments were noted there.

The 79-foot pilot schooner *Washington* was built at Brooklyn in 1884. Originally numbered 22, she became #5 when the number of pilot schooners was reduced from 22 to 6 in the mid-1890s. To reduce sail in heavy winds, the *Washington* has three bands of reef points on her fore- and mainsail, two removable bonnets laced on her forestaysail, and a bonnet on her jib. (Courtesy William G. Hagen)

The men on the Inward were assigned to either Eastern or Southern Station and went down in the sailboat on the 9:45 A.M. take-off or the *New York* ("Trolley") at night. A man on the Outward, assigned to a sailing, could get a man assigned to sea duty to "carry" his ship (called "getting an angel"). He then could go home and remain officially

The pilot schooner *Trenton* #4 was built at Essex, Massachusetts, in 1904 as the Boston fishing schooner *Kernwood*. The 87-foot schooner was purchased for pilot service and renamed in 1907. In 1916 she was equipped with an auxiliary gasoline engine. The *Trenton* remained in pilot service until 1934, when she was sold for use in the Cape Verde Islands. Here she is seen with a double-reefed mainsail and the pilot flag flying at her main truck. (Courtesy William G. Hagen)

attached to his ship until she passed the "Hook," maybe days later.

For many years Pete Murphy, who had his boat shop on the Killey Pond at the foot of Clinton Street below Bay Street, built our yawls, doing a good job. We boys learned to make wire hoisting spans and rope puddings to pad the stems for the yawls, which used 14-foot oars. The yawls were 15 to 18 feet long.

In 1908 spare boys entering our pilot service received no pay until such time as they took a "man's place." They then received $20 per month, and after six years, as captain of the New York, I received $25 per month; boat keepers received the same. As spare boy on the *New Jersey*—a wooden steam pilot boat built 1902 by A.C. Brown of Tottenville, at the southern end of Staten Island—I stood the 4:00 to 8:00 A.M. and 4:00 to 6:00 P.M. watch with the boat keeper. My job was to clean the wheelhouse, polish the brass, and clean the candle-lit yawl lights, which were boxlike with one glass and made of galvanized metal.

I stood by the yawl in boarding, learning to row and scull the 18-foot yawls with a 14-foot oar. I helped wash down, and, cleaned the forecastle where eight of us, including two firemen, slept. In heavy weather, diving bows under, this was a bit different from the Astor Lounge. All hands, when they weren't painting or cleaning ship, were subject to call, day or night around the clock, to board or take out, in fog keep a lookout, heave the lead, or steer. There was no 40-hour week or overtime.

It was a beautiful summer day in 1908, with unlimited visibility and a flat calm, when the Red Star Liner *Kroonland* came along at Sandy Hook lightship. She was loaded with passengers who lined the rails, waiting to see the pilot come aboard. Pilot Charlie Ackerman was on turn, dropped out in the yawl, and as he pulled alongside there was scattered applause. He started up the ladder, about a 25-foot climb, and about halfway up his pants dropped, and when about five feet from the top they were around his knees. Applause subsided, and a hush fell over the passengers, interspersed with an occasional snicker. Were they to witness a tragedy or what? Charlie was stymied: could go neither up nor down, nor pull his pants up nor move his feet either up or down. Finally after several agonizing moments some crew members reached down, pulled Charlie up, and brailed him over the rail and safely on deck. This was a picture to behold: Charlie's white BVDs gleaming in the dazzling sunlight, coming over the rail could have inspired Kate Smith's "When the Moon Comes Over the Mountains." There was a deafening applause and much laughter as Charlie made his way to the bridge, still holding his trousers, to meet the skipper. Charlie, who was a jolly guy and weighed 265 pounds, vowed then and there that henceforth he would play it safe and

With two apprentices at the oars, a pilot yawl comes into the lee of a steamship. Passengers line the rails to watch the pilot come aboard. (Courtesy William G. Hagen)

wear both belt and suspenders.

In boarding ships in bad weather we generally made a round turn, dropping the yawl under the ship's lee and if unable to lay there to recover the yawl, would make another round turn. This meant getting into the trough of the sea and rolling rails under.

But if we had our troubles on deck, all we had to do was look into the galley and watch the cooks juggling their pots trying to prepare food for about 40 hungry men. We had

While the apprentices fend off the yawl, the pilot climbs the ladder to the steamship's deck. He will then proceed to the bridge (upper left) to direct the ship's passage up New York Bay. (Courtesy William G. Hagen)

four Japanese men in the cook's department, and with spilled soup sloshing in the scuppers and the going rough they would always meet you with their customary grin and a few cuss words. The *Trenton* #4 had a Barbadian, Joe Turney, as cook. The *Washington* #5 had Fred Dionysius, and the *Ambrose Snow* #2 had Manuel Gomez, who served as wardroom steward or boy on the old USS *Hartford* under Admiral Schley. On our two steamboats the captain and mate stood six on and six off: 12 hours on watch a day.

Chapter One

These boats had white hulls, buff funnel, masts, and yawl booms, and it seemed to me, when we weren't painting, we were "sougie-mougeing" using stages and yawls over the side to do the hull. We made our own swabs using strings of heavy canvas. We made spans (wire) for our yawls, also the blue bunting Pilot flag flown from the mainmast truck, cock-billed there on a flagpole.

We also had a good searchlight, and at night, when a light hove into sight, we would direct flashes in that direction, and if that vessel desired a pilot he would burn a Coston signal (blue light). This system was gradually replaced by the blinker or Morse light. The *New Jersey* kept Eastern Station offshore of Sandy Hook lightship. The *New York* ("Trolley") kept Bar Station and was used as a trolley to go up for pilots or land them at 8:00 P.M. On the Southern Station was a sailboat with six pilots, cruising south of Scotland lightship with another sailboat called Inside Boat on the way down with six pilots. When the Outside Boat boarded four vessels, she would usually transfer her last two men to the Inside Boat and proceed to Staten Island. When

Pilot Charlie Ackerman stands at the wheel of the *Washington* #5. Presumably by this time he was wearing suspenders as well as a belt. (Courtesy William G. Hagen)

The crew of the *Washington* #5: front row, Ed Winters, boat keeper Bob Peterson, and Sam Libby; back row, cook Manuel Gomez, Dave Beinert, and Arthur Roche. (Courtesy William G. Hagen)

the first of these two men was reported aboard a vessel passing Sandy Hook, another company of six would be ordered off. The office got its reports of in- and outgoing vessels from the Maritime Exchange, who were connected with a Western Union signal station and tower on Sandy Hook. These reports came in hourly with clearances during office hours. This was changed somewhat when the boats got wireless and we got a ticker in the office.

The sailing pilot boats on station at night displayed at

Chapter One

The Barometer

*Long fore-told, long last,
   short notice, soon past.
First rise after very low;
   prepare for a blow;
when it rises high let all your
   kites fly.
At sea with low and falling
   glass, soundly sleeps a
   careless ass.
Only when its high and
   rising, truly rests a wise
   one.*

Wind and Weather

*A red sky in the morning,
   sailors take warning;
a red sky at night is a
   sailor's delight.
The evening red and
   morning gray are sure
   signs of a fine day, but,
The evening gray and
   morning red, makes a
   sailor shake his head.*

Squalls

*When rain comes before the
   wind, halyards, sheets and
   braces mind.
When wind comes before the
   rain, soon you may make
   sail again.*

the main truck a white kerosene light, showing all around the horizon. Sidelights were lighted and in place in the main rigging, but were covered by canvas flaps and displayed only on the near approach of another vessel. The official signal was the burning of a torch at 15-minute intervals. The torch was composed of a six-inch lamp wick ball enclosed in a round cage at the end of an 18-inch shaft with a handle running through a cover. This torch rested in a 20-inch can half filled with turpentine, and we generally secured it to the wheelbox abaft the cockpit.

A miniature torch about six inches long was placed on a shelf in the after companionway leading from the pilots' quarters to the cockpit, and when a light hove in sight, or if an outbound vessel might come in too close, the pilot on watch would, in the shelter of the after hatch, light the large torch held by the boy on watch. He then would mount the deck from the cockpit and swing the said torch in circles for about 30 seconds, then snuff it out by plunging it back quickly into the can. Any ship desiring a pilot would in answer to such torch, indicating such desire by burning a "blue light" or Coston signal.

We also carried a muzzle-loading gun about 30 inches long mounted on a wooden carriage with wooden six-inch solid wheels. This gun was secured abaft the mainmast, but rolled out the rail and lashed there whenever the occasion required. Black powder was carried in a five-pound canister, parceled out in Bull Durham tobacco bags. In loading, a fuse was installed in the fuse hole, the two bags of powder were placed in the muzzle with newspaper, then rammed in with a ramrod. I have been anchored on station south of Scotland lightship with the kedge anchor in a flat calm and dense fog with an incoming steamer approaching, blowing for a pilot. Fearing that he might not hear our bell, we fired the gun. Another time, anchored in clear calm weather with a steamer approaching five to eight miles away, heading up for Sandy Hook lightship and refusing to haul for us, we fired the gun, then put four boys, a blue flag on a pole and pilot in the yawl and pulled about a mile or two to get the ship. We got the ship and with the four boys sitting aft in the yawl, towed off the side of the Norwegian sugar tramp's side and knocked off a smart eight knots; it was quite a thrill. If we were on station and the wind flopped,

In the cockpit of the *Ambrose Snow* #2, Manuel Gomez stands at the wheel, Ed Winters is in oilskins at right, and boat keeper Joe Sullivan holds a spyglass. The others include Heywood and Ed Braun. (Courtesy William G. Hagen)

we would often drop the headsail and anchor with the kedge, which was a light anchor with a wooden stock, attached to a five-inch manila rope. The drum on the windlass handling the kedge had six or eight large wooden cleats attached around to give it a greater circumference for easier heaving. When anchoring under the Highlands in westerly gales we used the heavier anchor and chain.

The strongest wind I encountered underway in a sailboat was 95 mph from the northwest on April 23, 1912. We were inside boat and lay under the Highlands under a main trysail and head of the staysail. This was the one and only time that I experienced using a storm trysail, although the "old timers" who cruised hundreds of miles offshore were forced to do this quite often.

Taking the bonnet out of the forestaysail or jib was quite common. I can recall a beautiful calm sunny summer day on Southern Station, when the *Ambrose Snow* crew, after downing one of Manuel Gomez's pot roast and spaghetti dinners, were rousted on deck by our noble boat keeper, "Nosey" Peterson, who stuttered a bit. We soon found out who was responsible. It seems Pilot Woudrige, "Oom Paul," had asked Pete if he ever put the bonnet in the jib, and he answered, "No, Sir."

"Well," Oom Paul said, "now is the time to learn." So we trudged aft to the lazarette, where the bonnet was stowed, lugged it out on the bowsprit and under his direction, hooked it up.

His next order was, "Set it," which we did. Then, "Lower away—take it out," which we did, thinking we were finished. But that was not so, for he said, "Do you know how to put in the bonnet now?"

Pete answered, "Y-Y-Y-Yes, Sir."

"Well," he said, "put it in again," and walked aft. Suddenly air filled the sails—it wasn't a god-given zephyr, but the indignant heavy breathing and "cussing" of the Snow's crew.

The air was blue with such remarks as "the Pudding headed ----," "the Dutch so-and-so," etc, etc. After it was set Oom Paul inspected it again and, satisfied, ordered it taken down and stowed. By the time we were finished, it was coffee time and we consoled ourselves with some of Manuel's delicious toast and coffee, having lost our siesta but learned something we should have known. Oom Paul was a German-born pilot who rated A-1, was a strict disciplinarian, absolutely fair and honest, respected by friend and enemy, and, as I found out as I grew up, it was too bad we didn't have more like him.

It was some time during 1905 that the sail pilot boat *Ambrose Snow #2* was on Southern Station about 3 miles south-southeast of Scotland lightship. She was under a single-reefed foresail and double-reefed main with a moderate southwest breeze. It got to be 4:00 A.M. and Pilot Francis Yates called Pilot Charlie Onasch for the 4:00-6:00 watch. Apprentice Hugh McIntyre called the boat keeper and spare boy who stood the 4:00-8:00 watch along with the pilot. The boat keeper was getting his coffee, leaving the new spare boy, "Nosey" Peterson, on deck in the cockpit. Pilot Onasch came up the companionway which led from the pilot's cabin to the cockpit to have a look around. He had a speech impediment, and in the dark he asked Nosey, who stuttered and was brand new to the job, "H-H-H-How's the w-w-w-wind?"

Replies Nosey, "S-S-S- Sou'west, Sir."

"Yu-you l-l-little s-s-son of a g-g-gun, you m-m-making f-f-fun of me?"

"N-n-no, Sir," says Nosey. It ended in a draw with Pilot Onasch going below for his coffee and a slab of delicious toast made from Cook Manuel Gomez's homemade bread. When Pilot Onasch found out that Nosey, whom he had never seen before, really stuttered with no ridicule intended, all was forgiven.

Two tugs played a part in our lives in those days (early 1900s). One was the *Reliance*, Captain Patter; the other, the *Hercules*, Captain McElwee, both experienced "Hook" men. They would get word, via Sandy Hook, of a sailing vessel making New York and would proceed to sea, intercept her, and bargain to tow her in. We cooperated with these men and passed along any information from inward-bound

Chapter One

steamers about sailing vessels they passed.

During World War I, Captain Billy McElwee fell in with the German bark *Indra*, loaded with valuable nitrates from South America, down the Jersey coast and, with the British patrol offshore, towed her up inside the three-mile limit. It was rumored he got $1,200 for towing her in, a big sum in those days.

When we were bound up to Stapleton after being manned and became becalmed, either of these men might give us a tow and be rewarded by $5.00 or $10.00 dug up by the crew, or maybe a hank of bananas given to us by an inbound fruiter we had boarded. Other times, when we became becalmed inside the Narrows we would throw out a yawl, put two or four men in it, pass them the jib down-haul and have them pull away to help us through the anchored vessels to our usual berth off Pier 14, Staten Island.

There were times, though, when we tried to retard the wheels of progress. One sailboat crew, bound in, manned, with a following wind in the afternoon, knowing that if they phoned the office by 5:00 o'clock they would be ordered back to sea with men, were accused of towing three of Bardes' large meat baskets astern and not having their sheets trimmed to get the best advantage of the wind. Needless to say, the boat finally anchored, a yawl was launched to pull ashore (at a sluggish pace), the boys proceeding to Webers Hardware Store to telephone, missing the office by 10 minutes and giving us the night ashore. In those days some pilots living on Staten Island would order us to deliver, to their homes, bananas given to us by fruiters we boarded while on Southern Station. Sometimes we got a 25-cent tip, sometimes none.

Manuel, cook in #2, made delicious bread and rolls and at times sent some to pilots, getting $1.00 apiece for his trouble. Came Christmas and he would stay up all night making about a dozen plum duffs (suet pudding), each one weighing about five pounds. I delivered about eight of these, starting out with them in a burlap bag and receiving $1.00 apiece from each home and 25 cents for myself.

Whenever we got a night, all hands would row ashore at 5:00 P.M. and return the following morning at 8:00 A.M., leaving one man aboard to take care of the riding light and anchor bell in case of fog. My first night aboard alone was a bit spooky, but strange to say I wasn't scared. I was a kid

Chapter One

Sparring on the deck of the *Ambrose Snow* #2 in 1912, boat keeper Joe Sullivan boxes with apprentice pilot Henry Wood. Ed Winters is timekeeper (right), while Ed Braun acts as referee. Retired Pilot Howard Hill recalled: "Back in those days those guys were tough! Boxing on deck was common among the apprentices for entertainment on dull summer days at sea, and they fought until only one was standing." (Courtesy William G. Hagen)

of 17 and there wasn't much to do except read a book or newspaper by oil lamp; no radio or TV in those days.

Sometimes, if a gale blew up, a second anchor might be dropped or more chain struck out. You rustled up your own supper and breakfast except when the cook stayed aboard, such as Manuel Gomez on the *Ambrose Snow*. He got $50.00 a month plus some tips, and I used to take his full pay to the Post Office and send it Registered, Special Delivery, to his wife, Maggie, at 379 Hooper St., Brooklyn. The few tips he got from the pilots went to pay for an occasional quart of Old Crow or O.A.K.—Krugers own at 98 cents a throw.

On days when we were off for the 9:45 A.M. boat from New York, the yawl would row ashore to the float at the "New Dock," Pier 14, Canal Street, for the six pilots. Manuel liked to see the "tippers" come aboard, and we would kid him by putting the spyglass on the pilots coming out and count: Timmy Corcoran, $1.00; Wancky Yates, $1.00; Joe Russell, $1.00; Johnny Ronayne, $1.00—$4.00 altogether, when actually the pilots coming aboard were all nontippers. "Ah, nahts" was his usual reaction to the situation. I can remember one Christmas (we had the day off without a company) Manuel had also gone ashore and, returning the following morning, we found out from him that his son, George, who had deserted from the navy, was nabbed by the Secret Service sneaking out of a drugstore, against his mother's suggestions that he stay in. Manuel bawled as he told us of this in the yawl, and our eyes were moist in sympathy. He was a faithful servant, going ashore about six times a year, and his chief amusement was getting loaded on a quart of Old Crow. He got up every morning at 4:00 o'clock, made coffee and toast on the coal stove, baked all his own bread and rolls, and yummy were they good.

At sea the boat keeper was called at 4:00 A.M. and stood the 4:00-8:00 watch. I, as spare boy, was called at the same time and stood the same watch. The boat keeper would get his coffee first, and I shall never forget, after standing in the cockpit in the dark, freezing weather, blowing a double-reef breeze, how it felt to have him relieve me and send me down to get mine. I was a kid of 16 or 17 then, and nothing ever compared with this moment to get out of the freezing, howling wind to the shelter of the warm forecastle and get a whiff of good old Java and Manuel's toast as you came down the hatch. To sit down and quaff this nectar of the gods and wrap myself around a thick slab of Manuel's bread, toasted with gobs of butter, made for pure and unadulterated contentment, and if I had a tail I would have purred. After another short "shin roast" by the fire, it was back on deck until breakfast time.

In boarding a ship in this sort of weather, all hands were called. The yawl, which rested on skids, was turned up; the painter was led around the fore rigging; the stern painter, which lashed the three oars, was loosened; thole pins were put into place; and everything was made ready; then the yawl was slid along the greased rail and overboard. The two boys jump in with the candle-lit yawl light and emergency blue light (Coston signal) bag, then the pilot. Sometimes the yawl was towed astern to a proper position before dropping out. The yawls were 18 feet long, clinker built, with a center span of wire for hoisting aboard. The oars were 14 feet long.

We wore various and assorted articles of clothing in those days, none of them stylish: cast-off pilot's clothes, "Cape Ann" heavy slippers, or shoes, unlaced, that could easily be kicked off in case of going overboard. The warmest hand gear were the "Fisherman's Mittens" or Ponticas made of heavy wool. Reefing or shortening sail was for me at first an ordeal, and in freezing weather, unable to wear gloves while passing reef points, made it rough and my hands took a beating. One man had charge of the throat halyards, another the peak. Another was "tack man," who also stretched the reef tackle and secured it to the reef pennant. The boat keeper got out on the footropes of the main boom (45 feet long) and after putting the reef cloth in place to prevent chafing, secured the reef earing. Sometimes the sail was frozen from the spray, and that made it difficult to lap or fold and also to tie the reef points.

In my day we only used the storm trysail once. This was a triangular sail that was rigged to replace either the fore- or mainsail and was stowed aft in the lazarette. There were times in a strong easterly when we would transfer our entire Southern Station company to the Inside Bar Boat (*New York*) and be ordered to anchor behind the Hook or Spit. What a relief it was, when running in before a gale with heavy seas and with visibility limited due to heavy snow or fog, to make your buoys, and using the lead finally to get safely to anchor in sheltered smooth waters. How pleasant it was to get out of the rolling and banging sea,

The *Washington* #5 with her yawl and two apprentices astern, coming alongside to be picked up. (Courtesy William G. Hagen)

"snug her down" for the night, turn in and get a good night's rest and sleep. Standing a two-hour watch, while at anchor, I would pass the time fishing, sometimes landing six or eight ling (snot heads) or silver hake or fluke.

Later on, as boat keeper of the *Washington* #5 ("Mule"), my crew was Henry Mahlmann, Bob Peterson, Sam Libby, Dave Beinert, and Arthur Roche, with Buck Freeman, who relieved Fred Dionysius, as cook. My crew in the *Ambrose Snow* #2 was Bill Ireland, Dave Beinert, Clarence Esquirol, and Arthur Roche.

On numerous occasions during winter a sailboat's rigging, yawl, halyards, and sails would ice up due to freezing rain or spray, which meant we had to get out the ice beaters (old sawed-off oars) to rid the boat of ice. When the ice got running heavy in the harbor, George Stapleton with his little tug *Stapleton*, which also was a waterboat, would tow each sailboat to Mariner's Harbor to lay up until conditions improved in the spring. We unbent all the sails, repaired them, put the booms in the crotch, cleaned the water tanks, hauled the anchor chain on the deck, chipped it, white-washed the chain locker and ballast, also cleaned the bilges.

I'll never forget my first experience cleaning a water tank. Each tank had an oval manhole for entry, which can accommodate a medium-sized man, and inside the tank was a series of "washboards" which extended almost to the top to prevent sloshing and thumping when the boat rolled. These boards accumulated, in the course of a year, a heavy slimy coat of scum, which we scraped off with scrapers, then hosed down the tanks. To get into this dark tank and, once in, wonder how you would ever get out through that little manhole made me a little scary, and after about an hour in there with the aid of an electric light and extension cord I was very glad to get out. Some of the fatter boys had a job getting in and out and invariably wound up at Carey's Bar on the Terrace to rebuild their shattered nerves, meeting with various degrees of success.

Chief Engineer Savage of the *New Jersey* lived just up the street from our lay-up quarters and, being a swell guy, invited the crew up to visit him, which we did one evening. He was a good host and furnished us with ample liquid refreshment. As the evening wore on and the liquid supply got low, the gaslights started to gradually go dim. Chief Savage appealed to his guests for a quarter to put into the gas meter. Everyone fumbled in his pockets but no one came up with a quarter, and the lights gradually lowered and went out, and so did we after voicing our thanks. The timing of this incident was perfect, whether, by design or not. We trudged down the street, and on the way several of my still thirsty shipmates were wrecked on Carey's Bar located on the corner of Richmond Terrace and Van Pelt Avenue.

These hardy souls finally floated off and made port, saturated but safe, their navigational equipment not functioning too well. In those days our boats dry-docked at Burlee's (SISCO) at the foot of Richmond Avenue (eastward), and the principal thirst-slacking emporiums were Uhl's, Keuchman's, and Einziger's. Those "poor man's clubs" supplied us with five-cent beers, free lunch, and pleasant relaxation after a hard day's work with a minimum of debauchery.

It was winter in the early 1890s when a sail pilot boat fell in with a French Line steamship during a heavy snowstorm east of Nantucket. After considerable maneuvering they dropped a yawl with a pilot and two boys for the ship. The pilot got aboard the ship which then proceeded to New York. Meanwhile, the pilot boat wore around, then, after a short reach, tacked to pick up the yawl, which was lost to view in the heavy snow. After a fruitless search that lasted some time, the boys and yawl were given up for lost. Four days later, the French Line steamship *La Provence*, bound from New York to La Havre, sighted the yawl with the two boys, famished and almost dead of exposure, and picked them up. As a result of this incident, the French Line issued orders that whenever a New York pilot boarded one of their vessels at sea, a bag containing rum, wine, bread and cheese, and sardines was to be lowered into the yawl (in any kind of weather) to prevent a recurrence of a similar incident. This practice was continued right up to World War I, and it resulted in some interesting side play.

In those days the tempo of shipping and piloting was slower, some pilots being aboard the boats at sea for a week or more at a time and quite thirsty, their initial supply of liquid refreshment having been depleted. Under conditions like this, the "Frenchman's" arrival was eagerly anticipated by the brothers of the drinking fraternity. These pilots were not alone in their interest in the French Line food bag, there being considerable sinister underground competition from the "forecastle crowd," of which I was one. Under normal procedures, when we boarded a French Line ship the bag would be lowered into the yawl, which then would pull back to the pilot boat. Arriving there with thirsty pilots lining the after rail, the boys passed the bag up to them, and the contents were triumphantly shared by the pilots. This brought into play some of the clearest minds in the forecastle, whose problem was, how can we get the rum out of the bag and into the forecastle without being spotted? After numerous head-splitting sessions several methods were adopted with varying success. The most popular was Method #1: In boarding, an oilskin coat with the sleeves tied at the ends was taken in the yawl. After the pilot started up the ladder, the bag was lowered, untied from the lowering line, and, with a little hocus pocus, a bottle was extracted from the bag—sometimes two, if the operator was exceptionally daring—and slipped into the arms of the oilskin coat.

This action called for extreme dexterity because 100 or 200 feet away there might be 10 pairs of staring eyes watching him. The yawl would then come back alongside the pilot boat and the bag was passed up to the waiting pilots, who would walk aft to examine the booty. Meanwhile, the yawl was hoisted aboard and the boys would jump out with oilskins over an arm and proceed forward to the forecastle to cautiously and furtively celebrate, while wails of disappointment and anguish wafted gently forward from the pilots on the quarterdeck, disappointed at not getting any rum or wine.

Method #2 consisted of stationing a man at an open port, way up forward in the forecastle. After boarding the ship, the yawl coming alongside the pilot boat would land way up under the bow, the bottle of rum was passed deftly to the arm extended out of the port, and the yawl then continue along the side to be hoisted aboard. This method bilked an occasional nosey pilot who had the gall to examine the oilskins in the yawl for contraband—the nerve! Can you imagine not trusting us hard-working but very thirsty sailors? After all, the bag was lowered into the yawl to preserve the life of the boys at the oars, not the pilots. I can still see old Pilot Denny Reardon reaching into the bag, bringing out the bread, cheese, and sardines, but no wine or rum; with woe and anguish in his voice saying, "The birdee has flown."[7]

In pre-World War I days the pilot boat on Eastern Station—usually the *New Jersey*—would cruise east of Sandy Hook lightship, now Ambrose Channel light vessel. One night, with the wind fresh easterly, a one-funneled combination cargo and passenger ship burned a blue light for a

[7] Common Denny Reardon was a New York pilot and had heavy bushy eyebrows. Captain Denny Reardon was a New Jersey pilot and had a full set of gold teeth.

On the back of a postcard of this Milton Burns painting of a pilot yawl signaling to the Sandy Hook lightship, Edward Winters wrote:

"During the winter of 1910, Johnny Hauffman pulling stern oar and myself bow oar, heavy sea, strong Easterly wind, heavy snow, put Pilot Julius Adler aboard German S/S.

In going aboard Adler kicked the yawl light over, putting it out. Our efforts to light it were fruitless and our blue lights would not light. We finally pulled for and made Sandy Hook Light Ship and were taken aboard.

The Pilot boat *New Jersey*, Billy Canvin mate on watch thought we were goners, got us after daylight in the morning. Close shave." (Courtesy William G. Hagen)

pilot. She was the German steamship *Pretoria*. Jack Lyle was captain of the *New Jersey*, Billy Canvin was mate, and Johnny Hauffman and I had the week in the yawl; he pulled the after oar. The *Pretoria* had a lee and ladder on her starboard side, but lay "almost before it." After dropping us out with Mr. Julius Alder, the pilot, the *New Jersey* started a round turn. We got alongside the ship, with the sea rolling around her side, and Mr. Adler in making the ladder kicked the candle-lit yawl light over, putting it out. The ship was anxious to get inside the lightship before a midnight deadline, when new custom duties would go into force, so she proceeded. The *New Jersey* had circled well to windward of us, trying to locate us with her searchlight, to no avail. We tried blue lights, which were carried in a special canvas bag. They were a new type, lit by friction, which replaced the old efficient plunger type, and it was no go; we couldn't get them lit. The *New Jersey* got further and further away to windward, searching frantically, and it was snowing heavier now. We decided to pull for the lightship, which was visible now and not far off, dead to leeward. We made the lightship luckily; the man on watch being alert heard our shouts, and we went aboard, where we were warmed up with hot coffee. The *New Jersey* was out of sight, still searching, and it was hours later, around dawn, that we were able to make contact with her. Happy and I were given a dressing down, but we were really lucky to be alive, because we had entertained thoughts of scudding in before the sea and landing on the Jersey beach. How lucky we were we realized many years later, when on January 26, 1933, Pilot Hugh McIntyre was taken off the Black Diamond Line steamship *Black Gull* by Apprentices Peterson and Strandberg. After hours of scudding before huge easterly seas they landed at Monmouth Beach, New Jersey, and were drowned.

One beautiful fall day the *Ambrose Snow* was ordered off.

Our company consisted of George W. Beebe and five others, all good sports. The Outside Boat was full, and there wasn't much due, so we proceeded to Old Orchard Shoal. With me at the leadline (it was my watch) we beat back and forth, and I shall never forget those two hours and the casts—mostly "half two" (2-1/2 fathoms, or 15 feet deep). After soundings were completed our company prevailed upon "G.W." to proceed to Princes Bay, which we did, anchoring off Lemon Creek and putting our five sports ashore with the yawl to get some clams at Bill's Inn. G.W., who didn't like clams and was a teetotaler, stayed aboard. After an enjoyable evening our men poured back aboard, all happy and in good spirits. One man boarding the yawl fell overboard and was instantly rescued by his alert shipmates. We got underway at daylight and proceeded to sea. On side trips like this we learned plenty. Thanks to George W. Beebe and men like him, beating a 12-foot-draft sailboat in and out of Princes Bay and other places was most valuable to us as basic training, as we had no set pattern of schooling in those days.

On another occasion we were ordered off New Year's Day and, being Inside Boat, proceeded to Gravesend Bay with another company of six good sports. We anchored off the coal dock, pretty well in, where we rowed them ashore to make some New Year's calls. Johnny Hauffman and I had the week in the yawl and orders to return for the men later in the afternoon. It was cold and clear when we pulled ashore, and we went up the street to wait.

We waited and waited and finally an angel in the form of Pilot Antonio Canavale ambled along. Tony was excitable, warm, considerate, spoke with a decided accent, and limped. He greeted us and asked what we were doing ashore, and we told him we were waiting for our pilots, but didn't know where they were. Tony slipped us each a dollar, which considerable act lifted our spirits out of the "slough of depression." He directed us to the Pilot Fritz Harpenaus's home, where our company was "hove to." We finally rowed them back aboard and proceeded to sea.

These sports and others were pilots who did their work well, liked a good time, were generous and considerate, full of fun and tricks, and treated the boys well. Their yarns and jokes brought cheer into our (sometimes) overworked lives as apprentices and helped pass a watch quickly and pleasantly. Some of these men liked to fish, and I can recall again being Inside Boat—the Outside Boat being full—on a beautiful clear day with a nice westerly breeze. We proceeded to sea, hauled our pilot flag down after passing Scotland light vessel, then streamed two bluefish lines, one off each quarter. We sailed down the Jersey Beach at about seven knots, just clearing the fish stakes, which extended seaward from the shore at certain points. The sun was shining brightly, the fishermen enjoying their catch and later all hands eating them, nicely broiled by Manuel, our cook. Later the *Washington* #5 transferred her last two men to us and proceeded to Staten Island. We took over the station, having had a most enjoyable and pleasant day.

There were two fatalities just before my time in the boats. Jimmy Ayres was ground up by the pilot boat *New York*'s propeller. Oscar Van Albert, adopted son of Pilot Ivan Van Albert, while running the donkey engine hoisting in the yawl, got his head caught in the gantline surrounding the drum and was killed.

In my time, Johnnie Ferrie received a smashed forearm and elbow while launching a yawl from the *New Jersey* in a heavy sea. She rolled heavily and the yawl at the rail swung out. Johnnie, holding on, lost his balance, and when the yawl swung in it caught his arm, smashing it badly. It healed, but he could never straighten it out. Clarence

Esquirol had his leg broken aboard the *Trenton* when a towing hawser caught his leg; he recovered O.K.

Carl Huus Sr. was boat keeper of the *New Jersey* when I joined her in 1908, and he was a swell shipmate. Sometime before this, he was over the *New Jersey*'s bow on a stage to paint or scrape. At the same time the engineer decided to turn over the windlass under the turtleback at the bow. She had an outside exhaust, and as the steam was turned on Carl caught the exhaust of live steam on his stomach, passing through his shirt. He received severe, painful burns, which took quite a while to heal.

One beautiful summer day, while laying at the Long Dock storing, Gussie Bolt and her friend, Miss Sutherland, visited Carl. He happened to spy me passing his door, called me in, and made me sit on the locker between these two beautiful girls just to tease me and make me blush. This I did, to their amusement, not being used to strange girls yet, being a little over 15 years old. Carl married Gussie, a fine girl, and had a happy married life, and a fine family.

It was May 13, 1912, and we were in the *Ambrose Snow* in the Main Ship Channel just below West Bank, bound for Staten Island on the ebb tide in dense fog, with a light southerly wind. Boat Keeper Joe Sullivan was steering, I was lookout, Ed Braun and Hen Wood were on deck. I reported a whistle ahead, which sounded like a "Chicken Boat"—a small steamer using the Swash Channel while on its way to Philadelphia. Joe kept her off a bit, and suddenly made the "bone in her teeth," then the hull, etc., of the steamship *Delaware* off the starboard bow, almost head-on. I kept blowing three blasts of the foghorn, and the ship backed her engines full. With bare headway, she struck us in the starboard main rigging, cutting into us about two feet. If the *Delaware* hadn't stopped and backed, but held her course, she would have cleared us by a whisker, but in backing she threw her head to starboard and into us. All this happened in a matter of seconds, and we began to sink at

With the *Washington* #5 sailing in the background, the Merritt & Chapman salvage derrick *Monarch* comes alongside the sunken *Ambrose Snow* #2 in May 1912. (Courtesy William G. Hagen)

once. Captain French kept his bow in the hole, and finally we sank just west of the Quickstep Bell Buoy in about five minutes. Most of us lost all our clothes and belongings.

We cleared away a yawl and, along with our old cook Manuel Gomez, we went aboard the *Delaware*. Captain French took us up, with the fog still thick, to Quarantine, towing the yawl. Here we disembarked into the yawl and pulled to Clifton, where we boarded the pilot boat *Washington* #5 anchored there. Louie Schwarz had the night aboard and, when we told him the *Ambrose Snow* #2 had been sunk, he didn't believe it. He thought we were kidding.

In Court, subsequently, it was ruled that each was to blame, we for altering our course, the *Delaware* for excessive speed. Each, I believe, paid half the costs.

The *Ambrose Snow* was raised a short time later by Merritt & Chapman's derrick *Monarch*, Tucker and Narvik in charge, towed to Clifton, pumped out, then taken to SISCO's in Port Richmond. She was patched up, cleaned (some mess), and restored to service. In 1914 I was made boat keeper of the *Snow* and was the last one until she was sold to Portuguese owners in 1915 or 1916.

In 1912, Pilot Ernest Sloat was assigned to the schooner *I. Herbert Taft*, loaded with cement to a draft of 22 feet, bound to sea. While they were towing down the Main Ship Channel the wind swung around to the east, and the skipper decided to anchor behind the Hook to await a fair wind. After anchoring, the skipper signed the pilot's order and discharged him, saying that he was an old timer, knew New York Harbor like a book, and would put to sea himself when he got a fair wind. Pilot Sloat returned to Mohawk on the tug. Several days later, with a fair wind, the schooner got underway, sailed out Bayside Cut (Sandy Hook Channel), and piled up hard and fast aground to the northward of the inner buoy of Gedneys 6. Tugs tried to free her, but she opened up and started settling in the sand. She kept on until only her four masts were visible, and they in time carried away and were removed. The wreck was marked on the chart for some years, but it was eventually removed from the chart, the vessel having been swallowed up by the sands of the Romer, with the same depth of water as before.

Suspended from the salvage crane of the *Monarch*, the *Ambrose Snow* is ready to be moved to the SISCO yard for repairs. (Courtesy William G. Hagen)

Chapter Two

"My First Big Ship"
Piloting During World War I, 1917-1921

During World War I there were a number of U.S. government colliers in operation. They were twin-screw, with engines aft, capable of about 14-knot speed, with two athwartships funnels. Of these, the USS *Cyclops*, bound to New York with a cargo of manganese ore, disappeared in the Caribbean without a trace in March 1918. The USS *Jupiter* was converted into our first aircraft carrier, USS *Langley*, after the war. The USS *Nereus* and *Jason* ran coal on the coast for Cornelius and Boland after World War I.

During the war, the USS *Orion*, inbound with no pilot, Captain Hansen in command, sank the outbound British steamship *Port Phillip*, loaded with war materials. Her pilot was Anthony Canavale. She sank off Swinburne Island, a little west of the center of the channel and headed north and south. Several months later, Pilot Frank Butler was outbound on the steamship *Berengaria*, with a draft of 39 feet, which had sailed from Pier 54, North River, on the last of the flood tide. Visibility was poor, and it became real thick below the Narrows, with a strong ebb tide. "Butts" passed Craven Shoals and was forced over by an incoming ship. Suddenly, he found himself looking down on the *Port Phillip* on her port side. What a thrill! He backed full up against the current and miraculously didn't hit the wreck or the bottom. The *Berengaria* wasn't very handy. After considerable maneuvering they headed down and proceeded to sea, all safe.

About 9:00 P.M. on January 31, 1918, with a fresh northwest wind, cold and clear, I boarded the Belgian steamship *Anvers* off Ambrose light vessel, inbound from Europe. As usual, the skipper was glad to get in, the German subs having been very busy and successful. We anchored at Quarantine and went below to the skipper's room, which wasn't very big. We had a scotch and soda, discussing subs and the war. Adorning the walls of his cabin were numerous trophies, mostly guns. When I expressed interest, the skipper took down a small gun with a large-bore barrel, describing it as a gun used to fire signal flares. After that he took down a wooden gun case, opened it, and took out a German Mauser pistol, which could be used as an automatic pistol or could be hooked into a slot on the end of the case and used as a rifle. He handed it to me for examination and I asked him if it was loaded. He said it was OK. I fooled around with it, then handed it back.

He examined several others and finally came to a gun over his bunk, which he took down, telling me it was a Colt .38 caliber automatic and the best gun he had. After taking out a clip of cartridges and putting on the safety catch, he handed it to me as we both sat down. I asked, "Is it loaded?" and he answered, "She was, but she is OK now." I weighed the gun, discussed its superior qualities, threw off the safety catch, and pulled the trigger. BANG! The gun went off! I almost died of fright; the skipper turned greenish and felt himself to see if he was still alive.

The bullet had entered the wooden floor just clear of his feet and must have hit a steel plate, because when we examined the room below we found no trace. We had another drink to steady our nerves, then turned in, thankful that no damage had been done and that I had observed the number one safety rule—Never point a loaded gun at anyone.

April 23, 1918, was one of the big arrival days of World War I: 54 ships arrived. On board the pilot boat *Sandy Hook* on station at sea, we were down to four or five men with a large liner still due. Pilot Oscar Stoffreiden had the turn

The Norwegian whaling steamer *Hektoria* was built at Belfast, Ireland, in 1899 as the White Star liner *Medic*. The 550-foot ship provided passenger service between England and Australia until serving as a transport during World War I. Sold to Norwegian owners and converted to a whaling factory ship in 1928, she was renamed *Hektoria*. Returning to British registry in 1932, she was being used as an oil tanker when she was torpedoed and sunk in 1942. (Mystic Seaport, 1979.54.184)

when the White Star liner *Medic* came along. I had my deputy 23-foot license and the last turn, but he ordered me to take the ship. This was my first big ship. As it turned out, she was over my draft at 30 feet eight inches. She had four masts, one funnel, and looked awful big. She was partly loaded and had orders to anchor at Staten Island to top off with a deckload of horses. I started looking for a clear berth at Staten Island and finally got a clean berth way up off 149th Street, North River. In those days anchorages for drop vessels weren't too plentiful. What with the submarine net running across the bay from Quarantine to Brooklyn, and the Flats and North River not dredged, anchoring at times was a problem.

Twenty-three years later, on June 6, 1941, about midnight, I was put aboard the Norwegian whaler *Hektoria* at sea. She had two masts and one funnel, and she was a terrific climb, but had a good ladder. When I finally arrived at the bridge, the skipper said, "Quite a climb, Pilot!"

I replied, "Yes, but thank you for a good ladder." He then informed me that this was formerly the White Star liner *Medic*, converted into a whaler in 1932, and now chartered by the British Admiralty. I then told him that I didn't recognize her at first, but that in 1918 she was my first big ship and was like an old friend.[1]

I was at sea on July 19, 1918, on Eastern Station aboard the pilot boat *Sandy Hook*. It was a beautiful calm, clear, sunny day. About noon we raised a smoke to the east, and shortly after we saw a smokestack along with what appeared to be a large white bridge. This huge area of white was hard to understand until the ship was over the horizon and hove fully into view. It was the British tanker *G.R. Crowe*, and she was covered stem to stern with sailors in their whites; it was a sight I shall never forget. We put Pilot Oscar Stoffrieden aboard and she proceeded to port. We then got word that these men were survivors from the USS *San Diego*, which had struck a mine and sank off Fire Island with a loss of 50 lives. This made us realize how close the German subs were operating to our own stomping grounds off Ambrose, and made us wish for more of the 100-foot subchasers that were our main protection at the time.

Pilot Charles Bayer (UGH) slipped on subway stairs, breaking his leg, and when it healed it was stiff. He was a big and heavy man, but managed to get up and down ship's ladders OK. On December 24, 1918, in the afternoon, he got into the yawl to board the United Fruit steamship *Mutapan*, Captain Livingston. I went along with him, being bound back. We pulled alongside the ship and Charlie stood up to grab the ladder before the yawl fetched up on the boat line. As she fetched up, he lost his balance and fell backwards with the yawl span under his stiff leg and the foot of that leg caught under a batten. Under the strain his leg snapped.

"Jeez," he said, "there goes my leg; you better take the ship."

I climbed the ladder and, glancing down, saw blood in the yawl. On the bridge I met the skipper, who was a fine man and very much concerned, this being Christmas Eve. The pilot boat landed Charlie at 69th Street, Brooklyn. After many months, Charlie resumed work. He continued to work, and it was a long while before he realized the terrific disadvantage under which he worked, especially in rough weather. In view of this I could forgive his vile, grouchy disposition and his reputation among some of his shipmates that he was the lowest, meanest member of our Association.

On February 28, 1919, I boarded the steamship

Bound for sea, a Norwegian ship drops its pilot near the pilot boat *Sandy Hook*, on station. The pilot yawl is visible astern of the ship. A large liner at right heads for the horizon after dropping her pilot. The 168-foot, steel-hulled *Sandy Hook* was built at Elizabeth, New Jersey, in 1902 as the steam yacht *Anstice*, later the *Privateer*. She was purchased by the Sandy Hook Pilots in 1914 to replace the sunken *New Jersey* and was renamed *Sandy Hook*. The *Sandy Hook* served as pilot boat #2 until she was sunk by the steamship *Oslofjord* in the fog on April 27, 1939. Edwin Levick photo, ca. 1920. (Mystic Seaport, 1994.125.81)

Liberator, Captain Iverson, lying at 15th Street, Hoboken, bound to sea and to adjust compasses. I was carrying her for my good friend Henry Wood, and after clearing the pier we proceeded downriver with visibility about 1,500 feet and considerable traffic. We made Governors Island and shaped down for Robbins Reef, when I heard, dead ahead, the fog whistle of the troop ship *Aquitania*, arriving with returning troops. We stopped engines immediately, holding our course and ready if the *Aquitania* desired to pass starboard to starboard (rather than the usual port-to-port), giving her the deep water along the Statue Anchorage. This was common and accepted practice in those days, due to the fact that the eastern half of the channel toward the Flats was too shallow for deep-draft vessels. We passed several vessels anchored at the Statue, allowing the approaching *Aquitania* sufficient room. Her whistle seemed to be broadening on the starboard bow, and this seemed peculiar to me, when suddenly we made her, showing her starboard bow and moving inside the Anchorage area below Oyster Island.

She passed us starboard-to-starboard with ample room, but she struck a loaded British sugar tramp, the *Lord Dufferin*, which I had just passed and was swinging out with a change of tide. The *Aquitania* hit her just forward of the poop, aft, slicing her stern off as though it were a piece of cheese. Bags of sugar smeared the camouflage on the *Aquitania*'s bow and sweetened the waters of the bay. The *Aquitania* was swarming with troops, happy to get home, but I don't think there was much happiness on the bridge. It was revealed later at the trial that the master, Captain Charles, and the pilot, William S. Devereaux, had differed as to the correct maneuver.

Pilot William J. Crocker Jr., aboard a Timmins tug bound off to sea, was at the scene and asked the tug captain to put him aboard the sinking vessel, which he did and stood by. Bill went on the forecastle head and, with the help of the carpenter, knocked the pin out of the 60-fathom anchor chain shackle and let it run. Bill directed the Timmins tug *Mexpet* and the police patrol boat to shove her into shoal water at Oyster Island. She finally fetched up, bow out of water; the after deck, minus the stern, submerged.

The *Aquitania* proceeded to her pier, slightly damaged, and the *Lord Dufferin*, some time later, was taken to Erie Basin where she had her stern replaced. Pilot Bill Crocker was subsequently rewarded with $5,000 by the insurance companies for his good work. This money was, under our rules, divided and shared by the members of the joint Pilot Association.

The steamships *Great Northern* and *Northern Pacific* were built in William Cramp's shipyard, Philadelphia, in 1915 and named after railroads built and owned by James J. Hill. They were 524 feet long, 63 feet beam, 12,000 tons displacement, and had three screws driven by turbines. They did 25 knots and were designed to run between San Francisco, Portland, Oregon, and Seattle, beating the competing railroads between these ports. Both ships were taken over in World War I and ran in fast troop convoys with the *Leviathan, Mauretania, Olympic,* and *Aquitania*. After the war they operated in the U.S. Army Transport Service, returning troops from overseas.

On one of these trips, July 14, 1919, I had the *Great Northern* to sea from Pier 14, Hoboken. This was the trip that she established a record, and maybe Captain Doyle anticipated this, for on the way down at reduced speed due to barges and traffic, he said, "Full speed, Pilot?"

I said, "What will she do?"

He replied, "26?"

"Not yet," I replied. "Let's get out of this traffic first and clear of the anchored barges and scows." He was probably anxious to get going and, when he did, he made the trip to

Brest, France, loaded 3,000 troops, and returned in elapsed time of 12 days, one hour, 35 minutes. In doing this, the *Great Northern* shattered the Blue Riband holder *Mauretania*'s transatlantic record.

Later, as the USS *Columbia*, she was administrative flagship of the U.S. Fleet for about one year. She returned to the Pacific and ran there as the *H.F.* ("Hot Foot") *Alexander*. After 1925 she ran coastwise between New York and Miami, with Captain Zeh as master. When World War II was in progress, she went under British registry, and when we entered the war she returned to the U.S. Army Transport Service as the *General George S. Simonds*.

On January 28, 1945, I had her in to Hoboken with Puerto Rican laborers, thus piloting her in both World Wars. She was some little racehorse, but not too handy. In February 1948 she was towed back to the very same shipyard where she had been built 33 years earlier and was scrapped.

The *Northern Pacific*, returning with troops during World War I, took Pilot John B. Swainson aboard at Ambrose light vessel. The skipper told him it was important to arrive at Pier 4, Hoboken, at a certain time in order to make train connections for his wounded troops. They opened her up, proceeding in and approaching the Narrows doing 25 knots. Johnny ordered "Slow" to pass through the submarine net, which stretched from Quarantine to Brooklyn, with an opening of 800 feet from the Quarantine dock. The skipper asked, "Will we be on time if we slow, Pilot?"

"Carry on," the skipper said, and Johnny did.

The guard boat, the old monitor *Amphitrite*, was anchored just inside the net and had several of her small boarding boats washed from her decks; coal and sand barges were sunk; and ships were ripped from their moorings. I don't remember whether the *Northern Pacific* made her schedule or not, but damage suits were still being settled four years later.

The *Northern Pacific* was unlucky. She piled up high and dry on Fire Island while returning with 3,000 wounded troops on January 1, 1919. Again in the summer of 1920 she ran aground, blocking San Juan harbor channel for four days. She had General Pershing aboard for an inspection of the Antilles. On February 8, 1922, while in tow from New York to Chester, Pennsylvania, for refitting, she caught fire, capsized, and sank off the Delaware River.

On May 8, 1920, I took the British steamship *Strathearn* to anchor in the Flats, then to sea from Pier 1, Bayonne. She was a case-oil ship, and in those days much oil for export was shipped by the case from Constable Hook Piers. While at anchor awaiting papers, Captain Jeffrys and I talked about World War I, and he related to me stories of Britain's "Q" boats and their exploits. He was an officer in a converted tramp on Q-boat duty, with masked 4- or 5-inch guns, behind collapsible bulwarks, which were dropped when the guns were brought into play. The crew was highly trained; some of them dressed as women and all feigned panic when a U-boat appeared. They were trained to cockbill the lifeboats in launching, spilling some overboard, all with the purpose of luring the U-boat within gun range, then dropping the bulwarks and let him have it. Many Q-boats were sunk, but it was considered worthwhile to lose a Q-boat if they sank a U-boat. After getting out of Q-boats he became chief officer of a British tanker named *Vennachar*, later renamed *Wandsworth Works*. On a sunny day in 1917, about noon, while being convoyed by the U.S. Revenue Cutter *Mohawk*, that vessel suddenly veered across her bow, crashing and sinking shortly thereafter about four miles southeast by south from Ambrose Channel light vessel.

While I was on the French cable ship *Edouard Jeramec* in November 1917, reeling in cable for repair and replacement, we approached the *Mohawk* wreck buoy and found that the wreck was right on the cable. We had to cut it and pick up the other end for repair on the other side of the wreck. This was just one of the special assignments for pilots during and immediately after World War I. Pilot William McLaughlin was assigned to the 950-foot steamship *Leviathan* (the former German liner *Vaterland*, which was the largest ship in the world when she entered service in 1914), and some others had special berths. Then, after the war we had specials for vessels towing into and out of the laid-up fleet in Jamaica Bay.

During World War I, Port Newark turned out small turbine freighters under 400 feet long. Ft. Kearney turned out larger turbine freighters at the Federal Plant. Hog Island on the Delaware River turned out 110 400-footers. The West Coast, in addition to steel vessels, turned out wooden ships constructed out of beautiful timbers: green and unseasoned wood. There were experimental concrete ships, among them the *Faith*, *Sapona*, and *Atlantis*. The 300-foot *Faith* was built of reinforced concrete. The similar *Atlantis* wound up as a breakwater off Cape May, New Jersey. The *Sapona*, a similar 3,500-ton concrete ship, was wrecked on Great Bahama Bank near Bimini during a hurricane in 1926. She was used as a target by U.S. fliers during World War II.

After World War I was over, many ships were withdrawn from service, and what to do with them became a problem. Pilot George W. Beebe, in conjunction with Captain Parker of the U.S. Shipping Board, conceived a plan to put these ships in Jamaica Bay and at Pralls Island on the *Arthur Kill*.

In the Pilot Office, we established the Jamaica Bay Volunteers, with extra time off as an incentive to do this work, most of the men being unacquainted with these territories. Each ship towed down "dead" with three tugs, drawing 11 to 15 feet. Pilot George W. Beebe was in charge of assigning berths and was "Johnny on the Spot," putting in many hours supervising things in the bay. He also spent many a day teaching the rest of us the marks and soundings right up to Canarsie, then out to sea. We used the pilot boat *Trenton* #4, which by this time was equipped with two Standard gas engines. This was new work to us and interesting.

One nice summery day, April 6, 1921, I had the steamship *McCreary County*, with a draft of 10 feet seven inches, from 20th Street, Brooklyn, to the Raunt. We had the tug *Margaret Olsen* ahead, another small Olsen tug on the port quarter, and the large Shipping Board tug *Sampson*, drawing 14 feet, on the starboard quarter. We were in Jamaica Bay about a mile from our berth, going along nicely. Without warning, the *Sampson*'s bow rose out of the water, breaking the head and spring line. Then she swung around and parted the stern line and was aground, hard and fast, on a lump. This was a bit humorous, with us sailing away from our own tug, but soon, and without much harm done, the *Sampson* was off and back on the job.

On October 21, 1921, there were 122 ships in Jamaica Bay. These ships lay there for several years until they began to be withdrawn, either to be scrapped or to be restored to service. Henry Ford bought over 100 vessels for scrap, a number of which came out of this Jamaica Bay group.

Again we had volunteers to do this work, and on June 5, 1927, I had the tug *Baymead* in from sea to 69th Street, Brooklyn; then to Port Liberty, New Jersey, for coal; then to Pier 11, East River, for stores; then back to 69th Street for crew. We then steamed to Jamaica Bay, where we picked up our tow of two vessels, which we towed to sea. The tug drew 15 feet six inches, and she took her tow up the St.

Lawrence and eventually reached the Ford River Rouge plant near Detroit to scrape these vessels and convert them into Fords.

This was a pretty good day's work, and we all thanked George W. Beebe for teaching us all about Jamaica Bay, using the pilot boat *Trenton* for sounding.

Chapter Three

"I Enjoyed Every Minute of It"
Cable Ship Duty, 1917-1924

On November 3, 1917, I was assigned to take the French cable ship *Edouard Jeramec* to sea. I was a 24-footer at the time. World War I was on, with our country having declared war on Germany, April 9. This ship was about 250 feet long, twin screws, handy, and drew 17 feet. She was classed as a repair ship, the larger vessels, such as the *Colonia* (an old four-masted White Star boat) being called cable layers. Every cable is charted as it is laid, and with these charts to guide us we proceeded to place buoys as markers on the approximate cable locations, expecting later on to pick up the cables and repair or reroute them.

The ship's base of operations was Halifax. The skipper was named Le Martelieux; his chief officer, Tambon; his purser, La Franche; chief cable officer was Michel. I later met two French Cable Co. officials, Mr. Roosevelt and Taylor. These were fine Frenchmen. Skipper Le Martelieux had big blue eyes and a large sandy mustache. He was married to a Halifax pilot's daughter and lived in Halifax. Chief Mate Tambon was dark and formerly sailed on Elwell Mediterranean ships. He showed me how to work the eight-foot range finder, this being a very important instrument in cable work. Mr. La Franche, the purser, was a typical elderly French dandy with a small waxed moustache. He smoked one of "Ours" cigars (made for Pilots by Peter Makin) and enjoyed it so much that I gave him a box of 25. He accepted them and repaid me well by giving me five bottles of good liquor. Meals were leisurely and enjoyable, and at first I waded into the wine which was served in profusion, but I soon got sick of it and tapered off.

The day after placing the buoys, we returned to Staten Island. The skipper told me that he expected to work on the cables coming into Manhattan Beach for about two months. Later, when he called for a pilot, he requested that I be assigned to the job permanently. In this request he was supported by Captain Bayliss, head of the U.S. Routing Office (280 Broadway), who notified our office that any pilots assigned to this job would have to appear for examination and clearance. None of the men seemed to want this job, so I got it.

The skipper and I, along with the Red Star or Conway Towing Line's skipper and crew, who also were on the job, appeared before Captain Bayliss. He took my pedigree and I was OK. One tug skipper, born in Germany, was immediately ousted. This man was probably as good an American as I was, but this work being somewhat top secret, they were taking no chances; everyone had to be American-born. It seemed a bit unfair, but this was war. Other skippers who received clearance were Morty Fountain, Barnes, and Schwarz. It took a day or two to prepare a barge with equipment and gear for handling the shoal-water shore end.

We also made ready our own buoys, markers, grapnels, and replacement cable.

On the 7th of November we put lights on buoys off Ambrose Channel light vessel with the gun crew standing by the 5-inch gun aft. We later anchored the barge in Gravesend and sounded around Manhattan Beach. Then on the 8th and 9th we laid the two shore ends, running from the beach to deep water (18 feet) in Coney Island Channel. We used the barge, a tug, and a launch for this. It was beautiful weather, and I enjoyed the French picnic lunches we all had on the barge—sandwiches, vino, hot coffee, and fruit. We marked the two cable ends with buoys. We did further sounding, marking with buoys the edges of Rockaway Shoal in the area of the unlit mid-channel buoy and buoy 4 occ W.

In the channel at this point the soundings north and south varied four and six fathoms. But sounding east, with the tug drifting slowly in that direction with the current, we got six-, five-, four-fathom casts in rapid succession. Then, going astern on the engines, we churned the bottom with the tug drawing 9 feet. This southwest part of the Rockaway Shoal was charted at five feet and rose out of the channel like a wall. We placed a marker in 18 feet, which was important because the old cable we were to replace and remove passed here, and the cable boat drew 17 feet.

To start this phase of the job, we proceeded to a point about 800 yards northeast of Ambrose Channel buoy 2, dropped our grapnel, and worked back and forth covering a 200-yard area, hour after hour, also constantly taking bearings and cross bearings without success. We gave up and proceeded to the Lighthouse Depot on Staten Island, where Captain Yates, who was in charge, loaned us additional grapnels. We tried again, but failed. We then proceeded five miles to Ambrose light vessel where, after hours of dragging, we located the cable. In dragging we were restricted in some cases to 200 or 300 yards because of the danger of catching another cable, there being several in certain areas close together.

Not desiring to cut the cable at this point, we proceeded to run this cable over a sheave, slowly, to our original point of operation. On our run in we had to stop numerous times to ease the strain on the cable whenever our "tension indicator" showed excessive strain. This was due to the accumulation of several feet of sand over the cable on the bottom. A choppy clear easterly had developed, along with a heavy following sea, and I thought we wouldn't make it, but we did.

We cut it just north of Ambrose Channel entrance buoy

Edward Winters during his duty on the cable ship *Edouard Jeramec*. (Courtesy William G. Hagen)

2, placing a buoy on the seaward end, then reeling in the shore end up toward Manhattan Beach as far as we would float. Here we cut again, abandoning the rest. We subsequently picked up the newly laid shore end and spliced in a new section that we ran to our buoy off Ambrose Channel entrance 2; here we completed our second splice. The wind was strong easterly with a heavy sea rolling in, and it was surprising how the sea subsided as we proceeded back past Rockaway Shoal, which broke the sea.

We dropped the hook and laid the night out in a heavy snowstorm before finally completing our job. The cable splicer, Michel (a former Paris taxi driver), invited me to witness the splicing. Even the crew looked on with admiration as he did his work. As a preliminary of splicing, both the sea and shore ends were hooked up to instruments in the laboratory and tested. One of the instruments was a Wheatstone Bridge. Through resistance recorded on a scale, it could reveal the location of a break quite accurately, within a few hundred yards.

The cables were composed of various type cores surrounded by insulation of 1/4-inch gutta percha, thin, light tarred burlap, then light brass sheathing, then several layers of tarred burlap material. Then came the outer wrapping, composed of 3/8-inch wire wrapping called armor. This armor took the strain off the cable while being laid or reeled in, the water in mid-Atlantic sometimes being four miles deep. Any twist or fracture in the core would result in imperfect transmission. (The telephone cable laid across the Atlantic in 1957 had built-in amplifiers every 40 miles).

With everything ready for the splicing, Michel would join and solder the core sections with infinite care and patience. He then would heat the gutta percha to just the right consistency with his small blow torch, laying it on the core to an even thickness. He kept on heating it with his torch; then, spitting on his hand, he squeezed and worked the insulation, getting all air bubbles out. This, he explained, was quite important in deep waters where the pressure was great; an air bubble might explode and cause water and corrosion to attack the core, eventually distorting transmission. The outer layers and armor were then applied, the whole job taking about two hours.

When we were caught in fog, laying cable with the vessel underway, we would sound the towing signal on our whistle: one prolonged blast followed by two short blasts. While working on the Fayal Cable near Ambrose light vessel during a dense morning fog, we were sounding this signal when a destroyer, then a battleship, ranged alongside of us, missing us by a whisker. When it cleared we continued to reel in cable running about southeast by south. After about four miles we came to the wreck of the revenue cutter *Mohawk*, sunk right on the cable. This necessitated the cutting of the cable, which we picked up again on the other side of the wreck. We later replaced this entire section in to shore. This work continued until December 3, 1917, one full month and several more days later in the month. I enjoyed every minute of it.

In 1923 I again worked the cables from March to April 13th.

It was shortly after sunrise, December 26, 1924, that I boarded the British cable layer *Colonia* anchored off Stapleton. She was an old four-masted White Star Boat, and fully equipped to lay, full length, a transatlantic cable. I went to the wheelhouse, where the navigating officer was pouring over some charts. After introductions he excused himself and continued with his charts, going from one to another, using dividers and parallel rules, stopping at times to scratch his head. I watched for awhile, then ventured to ask him if I could be of assistance. He looked me up and down somewhat haughtily, then said that he was transposing cables from an old chart to a new one, and that things didn't seem to work out correctly.

I found that there was a ten year difference in the charts and when I asked him what points he was using for bearings, he said, Romer, Norton's Point, and the point of Rockaway. I pointed out to him that in 10 years Rockaway Point had made out about 500 feet to the west and also that there was a notation "subject to change" on the chart about this particular area. I suggested he take instead, the Barren Island Chimney, or the Rockaway Life-Saving Station. This he did, making out OK. He invited me down to breakfast, and the skipper not being up yet, he sat me down with him in the sumptuous dining room.

His name was Cockburn, and he turned out to be a swell guy. I ordered an omelet and toast plus the usual tea, and he had the same. I took what I thought was a salt cellar, there being several, and shook some on my omelet. He watched me, and said tactfully, "Pilot, you like sugar on your omelet?"

Seeing that it was too late to undo my mistake in thinking I had the salt cellar, replied, "Yes, I do," and with some effort, ate the omelet, sugar and all.

After breakfast we got down to business, and he told me we were to relay a 10-mile length of the shore end of the Havana-New York cable. This was being done to accommodate the contemplated dredging of Rockaway Channel, which the present cable crossed.

We placed buoys, anchors, markers, and lights aboard a scow and, when all was ready, Captain Mort Fountain of the tug *S.E. Vaughn* took us in tow and we proceeded down Coney Island Channel to Manhattan Beach. Here we started our buoys and markers, our course heading at Romer Light. After about a mile we altered our course to the South

Chapter Three

Telegraph Ship

*A telegraph ship whilst
working a cable,
To get out of the way
is clearly not able,
So three lights she carries,
all through the whole night,
Two of them red, and the
middle one white.
Her signals by day with the
night will compare,
She has two of the round
and the middle one square.*

and finally arriving at a point about 2,200 yards northeast of Ambrose Channel buoy 6. We changed our course again, heading to sea on a southeasterly course, passing about 1,200 yards north of the Whistler. After placing our last buoy we returned to the *Colonia*, having put in a full day. During the night, 10 miles of cable was loaded on the barge, carefully coiled so as to run free while being laid.

We started out at daylight on December 27th with a light southerly wind and clear sky. Everything went well, but as the day wore on the wind freshened and a light sea fog set in. Our course ran across some 12-foot spots on East Bank; fortunately we passed these before the sea got too heavy. The *S.E. Vaughn* drew about 10 feet and was in danger of hitting bottom. We finally squared off on our last course, and just north of Ambrose Channel Entrance we were hit with dense fog. We finished our run, thanking our lucky stars that our hawser didn't part, as there was a heavy southeast sea running now.

All during these operations, Captain Fountain, Officer Cockburn, Mr. Taylor, and I were crammed into the small wheelhouse until, by good luck , Mr. Taylor got seasick and asked for the bathroom. Can you picture the *Vaughn's* bathroom? Not very pretentious.

We wound up this Havana cable assignment by picking up the buoys and markers. This cable ran from Manhattan Beach across East Bank, then southeasterly to Ambrose light vessel, then turned south. This being Prohibition, the schooners on "Rum Row" anchored east of a north-south line from the lightship. Here they often fouled the cable, probably losing their anchors, and they parted the cable once.

One four-masted schooner from St. Pierre and Miquelon, Canada, arrived, anchoring just offshore of this line and outside the "Three-Mile Limit." She was deep loaded and after about a month, she hove up, sailed away, flying light, having disposed of her entire cargo of liquor. The rumrunners, who operated mostly at night and in the fog, used fast boats equipped with two Liberty engines, doing 26 knots loaded, about 40 knots light, and ran between Rum Row (where sometimes six or eight schooners might be anchored) and shore points.

Some of these nervy guys even ran into the harbor during broad daylight, with the shells of the 12-knot Coast Guard boats hitting some houses in the Bay Ridge section during the chase. They often passed close to our boats on station during the night, running without lights. We went to the assistance of one rumrunner who caught fire coming in loaded.

I was aboard the *Sandy Hook* one beautiful evening, coming on dark, when a rumrunner headed for Rum Row doing 40 knots was being chased by a small Coast Guard cutter doing 12-14 knots and firing his little 3-pounder. The rumrunner passed close to us with the two men sitting nonchalantly amidships and giving us a salute in passing.

Chapter Four

"The Value of Slow"
Piloting Between the Wars, 1919-1941

On a pleasant evening just after World War I, I boarded the laker *Brandon* at sea. Built on the Great Lakes during the war, her wheelhouse was way up on the bow, her engines were aft, and she was about 250 feet long, this being the limit at that time for vessels using the Welland Locks into the Great Lakes.

She was traveling coastwise from Savannah, Georgia, so we anchored on the Flats. The skipper invited me into his room under the wheelhouse, where we had a nightcap and shot the breeze. He told me he left Port Washington, one of the westernmost ports on Lake Superior, in the Duluth area, about two months before, proceeded through the Lakes and numerous locks, and down the St. Lawrence to Savannah, where she loaded cotton for her home port.

"You know, Pilot, when I get back home I have to answer to a charge of Piracy on the High Seas." When he saw my doubtful expression he went to his safe and took out a sheaf of papers. Selecting one, he gave it to me to read, and sure enough, there it was: "U.S. Treasury Dept.— Subject—Piracy on the High Seas." The skipper, an ex-prize-fighter, then told me that, while steaming on Lake Superior, a gale blew up and he started digging in for the weather shore. They came across a brand-new barge adrift. After some difficulty they put a man aboard and took her in tow, putting into the nearest port for the night.

The barge had broken adrift from a tug, which had to run for shelter to keep from foundering. The wind abated, and the next morning the tug captain located the barge and demanded its release. The situation finally developed into a brawl, with the skipper using his gun to chase the tugs off. He had demanded a salvage fee for saving the barge, which was refused. After the tugs' crews were held prisoner for several hours, a salvage paper was signed and the barge released, the skipper little knowing the mess this bit of gunplay had created.

"So, Pilot, I don't know whether I get the 2,000 bucks salvage or two years in the hoosegow," he concluded.

One nice evening just after World War I, I boarded the US steamship *West Celeron* at Ambrose light vessel. As I climbed over the rail, I was greeted by the usual, "Pilot, have you got any cigarettes?" Cigarettes were worth their weight in gold in Europe, and American sailors would swap cartons for binoculars, cameras, sextants, and other articles, leaving themselves short. I met Captain Griffith on the bridge, and he asked me the same question. I told him I had a box of 25 cigars and two packs of cigarettes, which I put at his disposal. He thanked me and parceled out the cigarettes, smoking a cigar himself with relish.

He said the ship had 1,800 tons of explosives aboard, and he had orders to anchor in Gravesend Bay, which we did. He invited me to his room, where he introduced me to his supercargo, a swell guy. "Well," the skipper said, "Pilot, you have been kind enough to furnish the smokes; permit me to furnish the drinks. What'll you have?"

I said, "What have you got?"

He said, "Anything from gin to champagne." We were safely anchored and our work was finished. We relaxed, the champagne flowed like water, and the conversation waxed furiously; we settled all the world's problems in the ensuing hours and without bloodshed.

About 3:00 A.M. I turned in, all my navigational devices functioning fairly well. I slept well, and about 8:00 A.M. I was awakened by several blasts on a horn. I stepped out on deck as Charlie Marsh, the Bath Beach boatman, hailed the ship, asking for the pilot. He said, "Pilot, your orders have been changed, get underway, go to Quarantine, don't anchor, and after passing Quarantine come back to Gravesend."

I told the mate to call the captain and get ready to get underway. He just couldn't get the skipper up, so I said, "Mr. Mate, you will have to take over," which he did. Arriving at Quarantine, we tried to rouse the skipper— nothing doing. After some delay, the correct papers were presented to the Quarantine officials and we were passed. We proceeded back to Gravesend, and the mate signed my order.

Charles Marsh later took me ashore, along with a bottle of champagne and cherry brandy the good skipper had given me in return for the smokes. This was the first time I ever got mellow on champagne, and I liked the stuff. The hangover wasn't bad, but upon getting ashore I had several glasses of water and felt as though I was starting all over again. I shall never forget the pleasantness of that evening: the good fellowship; the gratitude for the smokes I brought aboard; and the fine quality of the champagne, not to mention the quantity.

On February 22, 1920, I boarded the U.S. Army transport *Buford*, Captain Hitchcock, in-bound from Russia after delivering several hundred Reds (Communists) to their Red Paradise.

Sitting in the skipper's cabin that evening, I asked him about his precious cargo, which had included Emma

Goldman and Alexander Berkman. He told me that the first two days after leaving New York there was some commotion, but that all very gently adjusted in the face of the armed guard supplied by Uncle Sam to see that they had all the comforts of home. With Emma Goldman were four or five others who were quite aggressive, the rest being sheeplike followers and yes-men.

They all expected a gala reception with bands, parades, and the keys to the city when they arrived in port. Instead, they were met and escorted off the ship by a detachment of soldiers and marched off the dock. Emma Goldman was later assigned to taking statistics, traveling throughout Russia via boxcar. She later tried to return to America saying, "My America, my dear America, how I wish I were back there; anything I said or did was for the betterment of my Country." She died May 12, 1940.

Late one afternoon in September 1921, I boarded the Spanish steamship *Mar Cantabrico* at Ambrose light vessel, bound for Columbia Street, Brooklyn, after Quarantine. On the bridge I met the skipper, a big, heavyset man with a booming voice. I gave him several cooked lobsters and a newspaper, for which he was grateful. He told me the crew was at dinner and that mine would be sent to the bridge. I thanked him, but told him I wasn't hungry and would be satisfied with some coffee.

We arrived at Quarantine after sundown, missing our doctor, who would have to board us the following morning. After anchoring we went to the skipper's room, and he asked me if I liked music. When I said sure, he escorted me to a spacious saloon (she carried some passengers), and I was surprised to see a table set for me and a waiter standing by. The skipper said, "Dinner for you, Pilot," and I sat down to a leisurely seven-course dinner—soup to nuts—with three kinds of wine, winding up with anisette. I did not look for this kind of setup, but I could not refuse. As I started my dinner, the skipper strode over to a large Victrola and put on records, all opera from Caruso right down through Galli Curci.

There were several officers at the table when my meal started, and gradually the deck crew, engineers, cooks, and black gang drifted in to enjoy the music. What impressed me was the respectful way they conducted themselves and their amused expressions when the skipper, with his booming voice, would join in an aria or chorus. It took me about an hour to eat my meal, which for a freighter was outstanding. This impromptu concert continued for another hour, and no Metropolitan audience ever enjoyed music more than did this crew. They had been permitted in the saloon, which is generally off limits for the crew, and the reverence and enjoyment shown for the music was nice to behold. This entire event was a perfect example of good discipline, tolerance, and teamwork. Events like this made a pilot's job most interesting.

On another occasion, I was having dinner in the mess room of the Spanish steamship *Cabo Espartel*, seated with the captain and officers at one table. They ate leisurely, as is their custom, and after awhile the skipper swung an earthen wine jug with a spout over his shoulder, with his thumb in the handle, and shot a stream of wine into his mouth. The jug was called a porron, and at first I thought the spout was put in his mouth, but it wasn't. The porron was passed from man to man and finally reached me. Amid smiles and laughter, I tackled it and did fairly well, dribbling a few drops on my shirt front, but it didn't matter much for my shirt was blue flannel. The spout never touches anyone's lips, and these Spaniards got quite a kick out of my act.

Some Spanish ships carried steers, lamb, and chickens,

which they butchered as they needed them. I can remember maneuvering the pilot boat in a dense fog among vessels anchored outside the harbor, with bells ringing all around, and hearing a rooster crow. We knew at once without seeing the vessel that it would be either Spanish or Portuguese. Even though these vessels weren't very clean and shipshape, the crews ate well.

Pilot Billy Brinkman turned in one night on the Portuguese steamship *Fortuna*, his bunk being in a cubbyhole under the after poop.[1] He climbed over a bale of hay to get up into his bunk about five feet above the floor. This being summer and hot, he left the door open. He was awakened about daylight by a rustling noise, and looking down saw a long-horned steer with its head through the door opening, munching on the bale of hay, its long horns clearing him by inches. He was penned in and felt a bit uncomfortable, but with a little patience and several shouts he managed to scare El Toro off, dress, and proceed forward for a shot of Java.

The night was clear and cold, the wind strong northwest when I boarded the loaded sugar tramp *Rolf* off Scotland light vessel. I went to her open bridge, met the skipper, and started in.

The skipper asked me to come to his room just below the bridge, saying, "There's nothin' around. The mate is very reliable; he can look out for her."

I refused with thanks, but on his insistence I went. After giving me a close scrutiny and having a short one he said, "Pilot, will you give me an anchorage close to Long Island (Brooklyn) shore at Quarantine? You see, I expect a boat off."

I thought this odd, for we were the first vessel for Quarantine, with quite a number of vessels due to arrive, and to anchor way out in the middle, fouling up the

1. As no Portuguese ship named *Fortuna* appears in the registers, it was probably the Argentinean steamship *Fortuna*.

anchorage for other arriving liners, would have me damned good and proper. We finally anchored for Quarantine on the Brooklyn side and rang off the engines. The skipper invited me to stay up with him and the supercargo for a couple of drinks. I declined with thanks and turned in.

I had a good night's sleep and was awakened by the sound of voices and a launch coming alongside. I washed, dressed, and opened my door cautiously. Peeking out, I saw a launch leaving the side. I then stepped into the alleyway and met the skipper, who said, "Well, he was here and just left."

I asked him "who?" and he said, "the boat," meaning the launch.

I looked around, saw the Quarantine boarding boat alongside a ship anchored near us, pointed at it, and said, "Captain, do you know what boat that is?" He looked, and I told him it was the doctor and customs inspector. It didn't seem to bother him; he was somewhat plastered.

After awhile the officials came aboard, including Mr. Currie, a rather severe customs officer. While he was inspecting the ship's papers, the skipper came out with several bottles of rum and openly offered them to the officials. Currie gave him a look of scorn, refusing the bottle, and I thought he would give the ship the works, but he didn't. After the Quarantine officials left, I got the ship underway and proceeded to anchor on the Flats off 69th Street, where she probably got rid of the balance of her illegal hooch.

This story illustrates the brazenness of the rumrunners, who in broad daylight with the customs boat several hundred feet away, went alongside this ship, took off 10 or 20 cases of rum, and ran them ashore. The "junkies" (junk boats) who did most of the time were finally stopped from operating.

After World War I the United Fruit Company chartered

a small Atlantic fruiter called the *Stavangaren*. A Norwegian vessel with a wide open bridge, she was a little larger than a pilot boat and handled like one. I had her in one evening and started to dock on the south side of Pier 9, North River, with a strong ebb tide. We had the small Dalzell tug *Fox* on the starboard bow. We went a little above the pier, then backing the *Fox* we started in across the tide. As the ship's bow got inside the pier end, out of the tide, her bow swung to port, so I ordered the helm "hard to port" (the new command for this is "hard right") and full ahead. The quartermaster rolled the creaking wheel over, and when he leaned on it, it collapsed like so much kindling wood. It was a tense moment. We were moving and it came time to steady the helm. The skipper and quartermaster, flabbergasted for a moment, struggled with the remaining hub with no spokes to steady the helm.

With engines stopped, we got a bow line out and shifted the tug to the starboard quarter. Finally, with everything under control and calmed down, we all had a good laugh.

The Old Dominion Line operated ships coastwise between Pier 25, North River, and Norfolk, Virginia. We could set our watches by their daily arrival at Scotland light vessel: 1:00 P.M. on the nose, docking at 3:00 P.M.

Just after World War I, a northeast gale hit the East Coast. The *Princess Anne*, bound to New York under command of Captain Seay, an able old-timer, was making heavy weather of it. When off the New Jersey coast, the skipper was thrown and broke his leg. Chief Mate Barker, another old-timer, assumed command. He was proceeding on a northerly course with visibility zero, in snow and heavy easterly seas, whipped by gale-force winds. He missed Scotland and Ambrose light vessels and, overrunning his distance, continued on his northerly course until he fetched up on Rockaway Shoals, southeast of the point and not far from the beach.

All hands were saved but the ship was abandoned. She was a mark for years until she was gradually engulfed by the sands and disappeared. Some years later, Rockaway Breakwater was built just west of her resting place.

On a beautiful day in the summer of 1920, I was taking the French liner *Rochambeau* to sea. Shipping was getting back to normal, and tourists were starting for Europe again to visit battlefields or, in some cases, graves of loved ones lost in the Great War.

The French liner *Rochambeau* speeds down New York Bay on her way to sea. Built at St. Nazaire in 1911, the 559-foot *Rochambeau* provided regular passenger service between New York and Havre, France, until the early 1930s. She was sold for scrap in 1934. Edwin Levick photo, ca. 1920. (Mystic Seaport. 1994.125.111)

As we started down the last leg of Ambrose Channel, an officer came up and spoke to the captain. After he finished, the captain came over to me and said, "Pilot, we have a passenger who has canceled passage and wishes to get off with you. How about it?"

I said, "Certainly, but see that the baggage and everything is ready."

Sometime later, the captain said, "Pilot, we have opened a port and the passenger, SHE and her baggage are ready."

I said, "Did you say she?" He replied in the affirmative. "Oi gevaldt," I said to myself, "what am I in for?"

The captain put a bottle of cognac in my bag out of gratitude, and I proceeded down to the ladder as the yawl came alongside to take me out. There stood the passenger, an ex-nurse in the American Expeditionary Force. She wanted to visit the scenes of her World War I experiences, but upon reading a current news story of a ship sinking in the English Channel after striking a mine, she got cold feet. We put her trunks and bags in the yawl, then lowered her in. Once aboard the pilot boat, I tried to make her comfortable, but she got seasick. Did you ever try to take care of a strange seasick woman? I had about eight hours of this before the boat went up that evening to land us. She was grateful and polite, but uninteresting—no Clara Bow. A little charm does make an unpleasant job more palatable, doesn't it?

On July 10, 1923, a beautiful day, I boarded the tug *Gypsum King*, at Ambrose light vessel. Commanded by Captain Blizzard, a very able man, the *Gypsum King* was towing three loaded barges.

This tow was from Windsor, Nova Scotia, where they had boarded gypsum for the plaster mills at New Brighton, Staten Island. The tug drew 18 feet, the barges drew 21 to 23 feet, and the length of the tow was 5,000 feet—almost a mile. It was high water at the Hook, so we would carry our flood tide all the way in and hit slack water at Quarantine, perfect for anchoring. There was a heavy ground swell, so we couldn't "shorten up" the towing hawsers, having in mind Bayside Cut, the most common area for broken hawsers. We proceeded in with full hawser, and it was quite a thrill for me to pilot this mile-long outfit in the harbor.

We came through Gedney's, down Bayside Cut, rounded the spit all without any trouble, up the Main Ship Channel, and eased down to get to Quarantine at slack water. The doctor's boat boarded our tug, then each barge, while we shortened up while proceeding slowly. We finally anchored off Staten Island on the first of the ebb.

This tow normally went through Hell Gate and the Sound, bunching the barges through the Gate, but due to drilling and dredging there they had to come outside. These tows or barges were eventually replaced by the steamers *Gypsum King*, *Queen*, and *Princess*.

It was a Sunday night in the 1920s, weather clear, wind northerly, spring freshets running (about 5 knots), and the pilot boat at sea was very busy boarding the "regulars": the White Star liner *Baltic*, Cunarder *Caronia*, and many others, all for Quarantine. After midnight my father boarded the Lamport & Holt (Liverpool, Brazil & River Plate Steam Navigation Company) "Rio boat" *Swinburne*, brought her in, and, Quarantine being crowded, anchored off Clifton on the outer edge of temporary Quarantine. At about the same time the U.S. Army Engineer Dredge *Navesink* left Army Base Brooklyn to dredge along the western edge of Bay Ridge Flats. All dredges tied up Saturday afternoon and resumed work midnight Sunday.

After getting a load she maneuvered to proceed to the dumping grounds with a strong ebb current running. In doing this she got across the bow of the *Swinburne* and sank there. Some crew members were lost; the lifeboats of the *Baltic*, *Caronia*, and other vessels picked up survivors. Subsequently, the skipper of the *Navesink* got two years in the pen at Atlanta. He had instructed the mate to take her out, pick up a load, take it to sea, dump it, return, and send a boat ashore to pick him up at 69th Street about 6:00 A.M. This gave him an extra six hours at home.

The *Navesink* was raised with the use of a cofferdam, which was marked by a green flashing buoy. A Standard Oil Company of New York (SOCONY) tanker came in one night without a pilot and, not knowing of the wreck, headed inside the green buoy to get into anchorage. The pilot boat *New York*, seeing this, flashed her searchlight on the wreck and warned him off. The skipper came to the office and thanked the pilot for this good deed, saying, "And I didn't even take a pilot."

On May 26, 1924, immigration quotas were set by Congress. Annual immigrants from each nation were set at 2 percent of the number of persons of that nationality residing in the United States in 1890; after 1927 the number was limited to 150,000.

The above law created what we called "quota races," in which ships with immigrants would gather below the Narrows, waiting to dash across the imaginary line running from Fort Wadsworth to Fort Hamilton. Observers, principally on the Staten Island side, watched to identify the ships entering. If the ships were lucky enough to cross the line after midnight of a certain date and their immigrant members came within the total quota allowable, they anchored in Quarantine quite happy. But the ships that came across the line even seconds later after the quota number was filled, came to anchor, later to find out unhappily that they had to return those who arrived too late to their native country.

Can you picture the situation these regulations created? Maybe eight or ten ships would maneuver around on the flood tide below the Narrows, trying to hold their positions below the line, for to cross it before midnight meant disqualification. Pilot Bill Crocker once had the Ward Line boat *Havana* or *Santiago*, Captain Mike O'Keefe, before the flood tide. Red Mike, with plenty of nerve, was eager to dash over the line, but Bill warned him if he were one second ahead of time, he would lose out. Their ship, being twin-screw and handy, was easily held by backing up against the tide, and at the proper second they were able to dash across the line, being among the first.

Pilot Arthur Peterson had the old triple-turbine Cunarder *Carmania* under similar conditions. This was a good-sized vessel and one of the worst to handle. Arthur came in from sea on the flood tide, turned her head to the tide, and held her just below the line. At the proper time, he went full astern (she had about 20 percent backing power) and backed in over the line and into Quarantine. So the ship could be identified, he had bright cluster lights hung over the ship's name boards.

There were many disputes over arrival times, and I don't see how the observers at Fort Wadsworth could judge with certainty, on a hazy night, the identity of all the ships. A small vessel being blocked from view by a large ship would not be seen at all from the fort and would probably have to depend on his arrival time recorded in his log.

The number of immigrants arriving on the first vessels were computed, and when the quota limit was reached, the remaining ones were returned to their native land. Those ships lucky enough to get their passengers in often rewarded the pilot with a small bonus for himself.

It was sometime after World War I, in the early twenties, that Pilot John L. Hall boarded a foreign two-masted fishing schooner, underway inside of Ambrose light vessel. The wind was light southwest, and it was quite "smoky" (hazy). After boarding, the pilot boat *Sandy Hook* took off after a vessel blowing inshore. The schooner had fore- and mainsail set, also jib and forestaysail, and was fanning along at about four knots. When John got aboard there was one man at the wheel, but no one else in sight, and as he walked aft of the wheel he glanced down the after com-panionway and saw in the cabin below a number of Chinese, who grinned at him; there were 19 altogether. There was no crew, and John got some of the Chinese on deck, trying to find out where the skipper was, but he could learn nothing. John knew then that he was the crew—he had to take care of everything, steering, trimming the sails—and with the *Sandy Hook* out of sight he didn't feel too comfortable. He got some of the Chinese to trim the sails while he steered. Some of them built a fire forward of the foremast, on a metal plate, and were rolling dough on a stick and toasting it. They offered John some, which he refused. They did not molest him, but was he glad to final-ly make Quarantine. Here he had his hands full, lowering sails and getting the anchor ready and over. This was all done with considerable confusion, and finally the doctor's boat came alongside, much to John's relief. The U.S. Coast Guard was notified and took charge. Some of the newspa-pers made up quite a story, surmising that the schooner was in the Chinese-running racket from the West Indies, and that possibly the Chinese had overpowered and extermi-nated the crew. Another story, and more logical, had it that the crew, having the down payment of $500 per head in their pockets, rowed to the New Jersey shore, sacrificing the delivery payment of another $500 per head.

The sun was setting as I boarded the Japanese steamship *Atago Maru* at Ambrose light vessel, bound for Quarantine. After anchoring, the skipper invited me to his cabin, where we had a nightcap. He was quite proud of his ship, inform-ing me that she was all oil-fired, converted from coal, even to the galley stove. He was well educated, spoke perfect English, and was a member of the New Jersey Golf Club. He looked forward to getting in a few licks of golf while in port. He was the nephew of Viscount Saito, Japan's delegate to the Geneva Conference.

This being New Year's Eve, 1928, he invited me to New Year's dinner, and in that connection he insisted on taking me into the galley and showing me the new oil-fired stoves. There was quite some activity, including some men carving roses and other flowerlike shapes out of potatoes and other vegetables. These they tinted, along with cakes and cookies, in all forms and shapes. There were several large carp, with a spit running lengthwise through the body and resting on bricks, cooking on top of stoves. This, the good captain said, was to be the piece de resistance at tomorrow's meal.

We passed Quarantine the next morning, and while proceeding to Pier 16, Brooklyn, the skipper insisted I stay for New Year's dinner. After docking I was a bit intrigued, never realizing the Japanese celebrated New Year's as we did, so I accepted.

Max Schlanger of Barrett Towing docked us, and about 10:00 A.M. the skipper and I went to the dining room. There were about 10 officers seated around the table, which was heaped with food. They all rose when we entered, the skipper placing me at his left. He raised a glass of saki, toasting in Japanese. The officers and myself then raised our glasses, they responded by bowing deeply and making a hissing sound by drawing their breath. We all sat down, and then there was a sound of feet in the alleyway, followed by a knock on the door.

"Come in," said the captain in Japanese, rising in his seat with another glass of saki to greet the boatswain and his gang, and they repeated the previous ceremony, bowing deeply and hissing. This being over, the captain told me that everything on the table was a product of Japan and symbolic, assuring me I wouldn't go hungry. Sure enough, there were mounds of food, and if you couldn't see it you sure could smell it, including my carp friends of the previous night, which they must have sent from Japan, parcel post.

The Japanese are very proud and sensitive people, and I was bound to be polite, so what would I eat? There was fresh shrimp, salted shrimp, smoked shrimp, and boiled shrimp, the same with all types and sizes of fish. Finally I tackled the shrimp along with something that looked like light chocolate cubes, but turned out to be soybean paste. And there was soup; everyone had a soup bowl under his chin, shoveling the meat and vegetable pieces into their mouths with chopsticks, then inhaling the liquid with gusto. While I sat entranced at the dexterity of my Japanese friends, a plate was suddenly placed before me with steak, potatoes, and a vegetable. This looked and smelled good, but how was I going to handle this chow with chopsticks? Sparring for time, I thanked the skipper and finally said, "Captain, how do you cut steak with chopsticks in your country?"

He was a bit embarrassed at seeing I had no knife or fork and said, "Pilot, you shall have a knife and fork. You see, in my country everything is served cut up, so it can be handled by chopsticks." I waded into the steak, catching up with the others, who were still digging and enjoying the odoriferous products of the homeland 12,000 miles away.

Before 1928 Japan had a merchant marine composed of various types and styles of cast-off Norwegian or British tramps and a few passenger vessels. Many of these had British skippers or Scotch engineers. After 1928 Japan came out with a series of new cargo vessels, built in their own country and built well. The vessels incorporated all the good points copied from ships of other nations, mainly the hatches and cargo-handling facilities of our early Luckenbach ships, said to be the most modern and advanced of the time. They were all diesel-propelled, twin-

and single-screw, and handled and steered swell. These vessels were manned by navy-trained crews who did their job well and understood English.

Late in the afternoon of May 16, 1928, the auxiliary barkentine *Sampson* came along, towed by a large Moran tug. I dropped out in the yawl and went alongside this former whaler, which was flying the Norwegian flag. I climbed the ladder and, swinging over the rail, was greeted by men in street attire, speaking perfect English. One man said, "Pilot, let me take you to Commander Byrd." Somewhat mystified, I ascended the poop deck, shook hands with the skipper, and then was introduced to Commander Byrd and his four aides.

We proceeded in under tow and, this being Prohibition, we were shortly challenged by a Coast Guard cutter. In order to avoid a possible boarding and examination, I asked Commander Byrd's permission to use his name. He consented, and when we were hailed I responded with, "This is Commander Byrd's ship, the *Sampson*," and received a prompt reply, "Proceed."

He was a swell guy, and in conversation he informed me that he and his four aides had gone out to Fire Island on the tug to pick up the *Sampson*, which he had purchased for future explorations. They had boarded the *Sampson* from the tug, which then took them in tow. We finally anchored at Quarantine and the tug landed us all at the Battery.

The *Sampson* was renamed *City of New York* and was considered the strongest wooden vessel ever built. During her visit to the Antarctic, Pilot Joe W. Sullivan would roll up newspapers and magazines and address them to her captain, Melville. They would arrive weeks later and were greatly appreciated. After her exploring was done, she ended up in Chicago at the World's Fair. She eventually ran on a reef off Yarmouth, Nova Scotia, where she burned,

December 30, 1952.

Admiral Byrd established Little America on Bay of Wales, Antarctica, in 1929. On a 1,600-mile airplane flight, begun November 28th, he crossed the South Pole on the 29th with Pilot Bernt Balchen, a radioman and photographer, dropped the American flag over the Pole—temperature 16 degrees below zero—circled the Polar Plateau, and landed once to refuel.

On December 18 or 19, 1929, Pilot Fred W. Fendt took the Furness Bermuda liner *Fort Victoria* to sea from Pier 95, North River. He encountered dense fog below the Narrows, which he carried right to the sea. Arriving outside, he made a lee on his port side, just inside the Whistler. The wind was south-southeast, with a moderate swell and sea, the visibility zero. He shook hands with Captain Frances, who thanked him, and proceeded from the bridge to the ladder to disembark. The pilot boat *New York* had sent her yawl, which now was alongside.

Just then the outward-bound Clyde liner *Algonquin*, departing coastwise with no pilot aboard, loomed out of the fog and struck the *Fort Victoria* on the port side, just abaft the bridge, cutting a deep gash in her side. She just missed the ladder with Fred on it, and he climbed back aboard, proceeding to the bridge to help Captain Frances. They sent out an SOS and launched the lifeboats, getting the passengers and crew away safely.

The ship listed to starboard and finally capsized at about 8:00 P.M. Fred—who couldn't swim—and Captain Frances were the last to leave and ended up overboard. The pilot boats *New York* and *Sandy Hook* picked up most of the survivors, and the coastwise tug *Columbine* picked up Captain Frances and Fred. He had helped Fred stay afloat until rescued with the aid of a boat hook. Crowded with survivors, many of them "honeymooners," the *Sandy Hook* landed them at Staten Island.

The Holland-America liner *Veendam*, Captain Braun, was chartered to take over the run of the sunken *Fort Victoria*. The sunken ship lay in 51 feet of water, 1,000 yards from the Whistler. She was visible at low water and was a hazard to navigation for 10 months.

The *Fort Victoria* had been sunk near the Whistler a few days earlier, but her position was not accurately determined or broadcast. The fog was heavy, so as I took the Export Line steamship *Exhibitor* from Kent Street, Brooklyn, we steered courses (one of the very few times) and, arriving off the Battery, decided to anchor at the Statue. We stayed there till midnight Thursday, when it cleared with a fresh northwest wind. We got underway and proceeded to sea, passing the sunken *Fort Victoria* on our starboard just inside the Whistler.

At daybreak Friday I came on turn and was put aboard the Portuguese four-masted auxiliary schooner *Maria Palmira* about one mile north-northwest of Ambrose light vessel. The schooner drew 11 feet, and the wind was north-west, force 5 or 6 (17-27 knots, or 19-31 miles per hour).

The skipper told me he had been anchored during the fog, got underway when it cleared, and lost his anchor, probably hooking a cable. The motor was going "Full Ahead" but, being small, had very little effect. It couldn't even bring her head to the wind. I decided to use the sails and, being on the port tack heading about north-northeast we reached toward Long Island. After awhile, I noticed a U.S. Coast Guard cutter trailing us, this being Prohibition, you know. The skipper told me he expected an Olsen tug to tow him in, so when I found out that we were going to lee-ward as fast as ahead I suggested we anchor under the Long Island shore in about six fathoms and await a tow. I told the mate to get the remaining anchor ready, that we would anchor in six fathoms, and after letting go to pay out the chain easy, checking as he did so. With everything ready, we lowered the headsails, tried to bring her head to the wind, and ordered, "Let go." The mate opened up the windlass compressor, but nothing happened. He shook the chain, same result; then he took a windlass brake and hit the chain several times. Suddenly the anchor let go. He jumped for the compressor and screwed it up hard with the inevitable result: the chain parted.

The mate gaped over the bow; the captain, not exactly calm, kept saying, "No ank, no ank"; and I had visions of Bermuda. I asked the skipper if he had a spare anchor. He replied that he had, but it was in the hold. I told him to get it hooked up and ready for use, and do you know when it was ready? The next day at 7:00 A.M., about 20 hours later.

We set the headsails and, with the motor running steadily, tried to tack with no success. We then wore around and headed about south by west, making more leeway than headway. The wind now was more westerly and stronger, and the Coast Guard cutter kept dogging our tracks. At three o'clock that afternoon we were about 12 miles east of Ambrose light vessel. The cutter drew alongside to windward and put out a longboat manned by six men. They pulled under our quarter, came alongside our port midsection, and put two officers aboard.

Lieutenant Brooks came aboard to inspect the ship's papers and manifest, which the captain produced and were examined. He asked if there was any liquor aboard, and the skipper replied in the affirmative, and offered him some. This, of course, was met with a polite refusal and a request for a liquor manifest or list. As none was forthcoming, a dispute arose; the skipper appealed to me in his broken English to explain and clear up this situation. It was outside of my province to interfere so I asked the lieutenant's permission to comment. I told him that, as far as I knew, under Portuguese law a certain quantity of wine was required as a daily ration for each member of the crew. All ships made up their liquor list for submission to the Customs boarding officer at Quarantine, after the pilot boarded the ship entering the harbor from sea.

This was the complete list of all liquor on board, which said liquor must be put into one area and sealed by the boarding officer, who then took the list with him. It was finally straightened out, with the officers returning to their cutter.

Later on, as the sun was setting, the cutter came up on our weather quarter and hailed us, saying, "Stand by to take a line." Pleased by this turn of events, I ranged the shivering crew along the pipe rail on the bow. The cutter came up about 100 feet to windward of us and shot a line, which missed. They fired a second line, which landed. We started to haul in several hundred feet of Lyle gun line, attached to which was a four-inch running line. At first I thought this was our towing hawser, and with the cutter drawing 16 or 17 feet while our draft was 11 feet, our drift was twice that of hers.

As the distance between the vessels increased we no longer could haul the line in by hand, so we had to take it to the windlass and heave away. It was dark now, and the cutter helped us with her flood- and searchlight. In this light I spied the end of the running line made fast to a huge eye: the end of a 12- or 14-inch towing hawser. We were now hundreds of feet apart and the heaving was heavy. We finally got the eye to the ship's side, but the chock, which guided the running line, would not accommodate this huge eye and hawser, so we took a five-inch dock line, formed a bight around the hawser, and made it fast across the deck to the port bitts to serve as a chock. Because the windlass drum was too small, we had to use 12-foot-long straps on the hawser to heave, inch by inch. Suddenly, someone spoke to me from behind saying, "Can we help you, buddy?" I turned around in surprise, and there stood six Coast Guard boys in their parkas. They had been sent over via longboat, and I hadn't even seen them come alongside. They were nice willing boys and helped, spelling the regular crew, who by this time were frozen and tired.

We finally got enough hawser aboard to take several turns around the foremast with a half hitch. We then lashed the eye to the standing part. Thankful that this task had been accomplished, we wondered how we could let the cutter know that we were "all fast." There being no flashlight available, I instructed the junior lieutenant to use a kerosene riding light to send a Morse code message to the cutter, making dots and dashes by using his coat to block off the light.

Finally the message got across and the tow began. It was now 9:00 P.M. and it had taken four and a half hours to get the hawser aboard. It was clear, with a strong westerly wind, and Ambrose light vessel was visible many miles away. We towed along at about six knots, and all hands had a chance for a rest and a "shin roast." No one had eaten for many hours, so I asked the skipper if he had any food at all for the Coast Guard boys, who had helped us so much. He said there was no food at all. I then asked him about coffee; he said there was some, so I suggested to give them plenty—which he did. The boys were offered wine or brandy numerous times and each refused, being disciplined and conducting themselves as gentlemen.

We towed well, passing Ambrose light vessel and the Whistler, and entering Ambrose Channel, where Olsen's tug *Revere*, Captain Bob Raynor, came alongside. It was now about 1:00 A.M. Saturday as Bob came aboard and told me he had orders to tow the vessel in and that he had the ship's agent aboard. He returned to his tug, and the agent introduced himself and started to step aboard from the tug. The lieutenant told him he could not come aboard. The agent then tried to pass some papers and letters aboard, but was prevented from doing so. The agent said he had hired the tug to do the towing and asked the lieutenant to turn the vessel over to the tug. That was refused. After a few more exchanges the tug left the side to speak the cutter out ahead, with the same results. Suddenly I suspected that we had been seized as a possible rumrunner, this being Prohibition.

We continued towing up Ambrose Channel right on the range, crowding the outward-bound *Olympic*, *Eastern Prince*, and *Bergensfjord*, which had left their piers after midnight. Their pilots must have cursed us for clogging up the channel. We finally reached Gravesend Bay, shortened hawser, and the cutter held us there, laying head-to a strong northwest wind. After daybreak the tug Revere proceeded to Quarantine and quite some time later returned with the doctor and Customs and Immigration officers.

The doctor didn't have much to do, and when the Customs officer asked the skipper for his papers he was informed that the Coast Guard lieutenant had taken them aboard the cutter. Their work finished, the agent ordered Bob Raynor to take the boarding officers back to Quarantine. Seeing this, I said to the agent, "How about taking me. This vessel being seized, there isn't anything more for me to do." The skipper signed my order for pilotage on an 11-foot draft, and we proceeded to Quarantine, where we landed.

I phoned the office and was informed that I was five on turn (my turn being 7:00 A.M. the previous day) and might get a ship sailing. I looked awful, hadn't washed or shaved, and was dead tired, so told the officer I was going home, which I did. It was now 2:00 P.M. Saturday, and when I called the office at 5:00 luckily I got a sailing for the next morning. I had been on the job from 7:00 A.M. Friday until 1:00 P.M. Saturday and I was pooped. I believe that subsequently the U.S. government had to recompense the *Maria Palmira* for damages and expenses incurred in what turned out to be an illegal seizure.

On March 25, 1930, I was assigned to the new diesel-powered fishing trawler *Flow*, laying at the Fulton Fish Market, Pier 18, East River. My orders were to take her to sea, somewhere within five miles of Rockaway. From there we were to broadcast the Forty Fathom Fish program, MC'd by Ted Husing over radio station WABC. This program was to be received at Rockaway and relayed or rebroadcast from there. The weather was clear in the Upper Bay, with dense fog, heavy seas, and strong southeast winds outside of Sandy Hook.

I boarded the ship and met Ted Husing, who had with him a crew of about 20 men, including actor, Captain Haff, the captain's son Peter, and Rubinoff with his violin. On board also were technicians with all of their broadcast gear and cameras. Captain Bryant was skipper and Mr. Mudge, vice president of Forty Fathom Fish, was also aboard. After rounding up the ship's crew from the various thirst-slacking emporiums on South Street (this was Prohibition, you know), we sailed. The *Flow* had steam-powered steering gear—quite an improvement over the other older trawlers which had hand gear—and in order to get the wheel hard over the engines had to be slowed down or stopped.

We hit the fog just below the Narrows, and it was dense with a fresh southeast wind. I told Mr. Mudge that it was impossible to do the broadcast at sea and suggested doing it in the sheltered waters of Gravesend Bay. He agreed, saying that this was costing the company $10,000 and he didn't want to muff it. I got well over toward Ulmer Park in order to avoid all ship traffic so we wouldn't need to blow the whistle once the broadcast got underway. All the broadcast gear was on the small bridge almost directly under the whistle, the sounding of which would throw the delicate instruments out of kilter.

We started broadcasting with Captain Haff sitting on a hatch telling yarns to his boy Peter, who sat on his knee. The chorus sang chanteys and Rubinoff fiddled. The grand finale came when a large net filled with fish was lowered over the side. With everything ready, the net was slowly lifted aboard, with the chorus in oilskins singing chanteys, assisted in some degree by the ship's crew in some bewilderment and wooziness.

When the net landed on deck, the actors, singing, were to swing into it and remove the fish from the net with their bare hands. This of course was obnoxious, and one man grabbed a gaff hook and started to use it. Mr. Mudge motioned frantically not to use it, because those were supposed to be live fish coming aboard at sea; no hooks were allowed according to ASPCA rules. The actors and camera carried on, and the scene was finished.

By this time we had drifted into the steamship lane toward Craven Shoal, and I heard the Old Dominion Boat coming in through the still dense fog. I recognized the whistle, and without thinking I blew our air whistle, almost overhead. It was a shrill blast and caused a commotion among our broadcast boys, who found that part of their delicate apparatus was put out of commission. They quickly located the break in this hairlike part with a microscope on a traveler and in jig time repaired it.

Having completed our mission, we proceeded back to Pier 18, East River, it still being clear in the Upper Bay. Mr.

Mudge asked me to stay aboard and do another broadcast in the evening. I expressed the opinion that after dark the fog would roll in and cover the Upper Bay, and pointed to the fog gradually descending along the big buildings. With this in mind, we could not be out in the bay without ringing the bell or blowing the whistle, due to barge and ferry traffic. Mr. Mudge agreed and so, much to the relief of the skipper, who didn't enjoy all these monkeyshines anyway, we stayed at the dock. It was dense all night, clearing the next day. Then, with a northwest wind, the broadcast was completed. I later received a nice letter from Mr. Mudge, thanking me for my advice and assistance in making the broadcast possible under adverse conditions.

On August 7, 1930, at 7:15 P.M., I boarded the Cunard line steamship *Mauretania* at Ambrose light vessel, with a light southwest wind and hazy skies on the last of the flood tide. Previously, we had put Dewey McIntyre on a loaded Mallory tanker, Erhardt Smith on Prince boat, and Dave Beinert on the French liner *DeGrasse*. I overhauled and passed Smith, then Beinert who was doing 17 knots, then McIntyre in the tanker at buoy 10, Ambrose Channel.

We had been hooked up 25 knots, but this speed was not apparent until, looking astern, I saw the sea washing across the tanker's deck, and further back tremendous seas washing over the East Bank light station and, with the last of the flood tide, headed for Coney Island beaches. I slowed down at once, and if I could have gotten down off the bridge and tramped down those seas, I would have done so. I knew they would eventually pile up on the beaches, endangering life and property. We anchored for Quarantine, and after getting pratique, proceeded to Pier 54, North River, where we docked at 10:15 P.M.. This was exceptionally good time, but I was worried.

I felt like a doomed man waiting for that knock on the

The Cunard liner *Mauretania* held the Blue Riband as the fastest transatlantic liner from 1907 to 1929. The 790-foot ship, launched at Newcastle, England, in 1907, had four turbine-driven screws that gave her a working speed of 25 knots. At the time Edward Winters piloted her, this extremely popular liner had accommodations for 1,756 passengers. Scrapped in 1935, she was replaced by the second *Mauretania* in 1939. Morris Rosenfeld photo. (1984.187.4699S, © Mystic Seaport, Rosenfeld Collection)

door, and finally it came via telephone. It was Harry Arnold, our president, who told me the Sea Gate Association had registered a complaint and I must stand trial before the Pilots' Commission. I appeared before them; they read the complaint and asked for my story, which I gave them in detail. They informed me that several tremendous rollers hit the beaches, but—warned beforehand by alert lifeguards—men, women, children, and babies in carriages had been cleared from the beaches, up toward the boardwalk. By the time the seas hit, the *Mauretania* was at Quarantine, out of sight. I assured the commissioners I had learned a valuable lesson. I was very lucky that there was no loss of life or property damage. I realize now, more than ever, the value of "Slow" on the ship's telegraph.

Later on, I saw a model of the *Mauretania*, and her hull was a thing of beauty: a fine bow and full waist, tapering fine to the stern. Standing on her bridge, looking down at the water while doing 25 knots, there was no bow wave. Her captain told me that doing full speed, she squatted down four feet in the open sea and eight feet in shoal water.

The *Fort Victoria* wreck remained a hazard until a wrecking company placed about 100 tons of dynamite around the wreck and set it off on October 16, 1930. There was another blast October 23rd. After these blasts, the wreck disappeared and normal traffic resumed. The day of the first blast, I was ordered by the U.S. Coast Guard to heave to in Ambrose Channel on a Spanish steamship. All traffic stopped. It was quite an explosion on a beautiful clear day, and the water and debris reached into the air about 500 feet. The wreck was officially pronounced clear on October 14, 1932.

The North German Lloyd liner *Europa* arrived one night from a southern cruise with good visibility but the wind blowing an easterly gale, with tremendous seas. Both pilot boats were forced to run in, one of the very few times in history that there was no boat on station. Captain Johnson lay off Ambrose light vessel for awhile, then decided to take his ship in himself, without a pilot.

He proceeded in with a huge following sea, passed the Whistler, and for some reason wound up hard and fast ashore, between Gedney and Ambrose Channel. At daybreak, after the storm abated, the pilot boat *Sandy Hook* put Pilot Richard J. Bigley aboard.

He reached the bridge and met Captain Johnson, expecting surely to be blamed for this situation, but the skipper showed what a fine man he was by taking the blame himself. He said, "Pilot, I always thought New York was a simple port to enter, compared to some of the others I have been to, so finding no pilot on station, I decided to come in by myself. So, here I am. I don't blame your boats for not being on station in such terrific weather." The Europa was refloated shortly after with the aid of several tugs and proceeded to port.

The *Europa* had two in-turning and two out-turning propellers to reduce vibration. The *Bremen*, her sister ship, had four out-turning propellers and handled swell. The *Europa* was awarded to U.S. after World War II; we turned her over to France who renamed her *Liberte*. Completely reconditioned, she broke adrift from her moorings in Le Havre, landed on the wreck of the burned and capsized liner *Paris*, and sank. Later she was refloated, reconditioned, and restored to transatlantic service.

It was some time in the 1930s that the *Europa* left Pier 4 (Army Base), Brooklyn, at midnight, bound for Europe. It was a pleasant night, and the ship was entering Ambrose Channel when coffee and sandwiches were brought to the bridge. The chief steward spoke to Captain Johnson, a fine and able man, who then approached the pilot. He said, "Pilot, the chief steward reports that we have several visitors who did not leave the ship. You will take them off with you when you leave."

The pilot replied, "Sorry Captain, we are forbidden to take anyone off."

"But," the captain said, "you always take them off; why not now? Anyhow, this is the famous dancer Marilyn Miller, and some of her friends. Surely you won't refuse them, will you?"

The pilot replied, "Sorry, Captain, but I am only complying with a new regulation, which forbids pilots to take anyone with them. For years, as a favor to the steamship companies, we have taken people off at no cost, but the practice has grown to such an extent that it had to be stopped. Careless or inconsiderate people, some in various stages of inebriation, would deliberately ignore the 'All Ashore' call, saying, 'Oh, we'll get off with the pilot,' and continue their farewell party. We are responsible for their safety going down the ladder and aboard the pilot boat, where we feed them and run the boat up to land them, all free of charge. Sorry, Captain."

Chapter Four

So Marilyn Miller and her friends (I think there were three or four of them) took an unscheduled trip to Europe.

Monday, February 23, 1931, was a beautiful day. I had just cleared Quarantine with the Dutch steamship *Veendam* and was proceeding to Pier 95, North River. She was under charter to the Furness Bermuda Line, replacing the sunken *Fort Victoria*, whose former skipper, Captain Frances, was on the bridge with me. Captain Braun, the *Veendam*'s regular skipper, was also there, and we were proceeding up toward Owl's Head buoy at about 12 knots against a strong ebb tide, when the steward came with some tea.

Ahead of us was a fast Japanese steamship, doing about 15 knots, rounding Owl's Head buoy. We were approaching port to port, and I told Captain Braun I would have my tea after clearing the other ship. It was good I said this, for just then I heard the air whistle alarm of the other ship, which kept coming left. I immediately stopped the engines and rang them up "Full Astern." The Japanese steamer let go both anchors, and you should have seen the sparks fly. We stood by our anchors, but held them and watched him swing to his. He was broadside across our bow, about 200 feet away, when we started to gather stern board, and he started to swing fast towards us, our bow pointing at his bridge. We barely backed clear when he brought up on his anchor. It probably helped us that we did not let go of our anchors. After we cleared, and the passengers who had crowded on the deck below and forward of the bridge to watch the fireworks had calmed down, we proceeded to our pier.

Captain Frances came over to me and said, "This is one way how not to grow old." I agreed with him. Strange to say, I wasn't very excited. Fred Fendt was pilot of the Japanese vessel, and when I met him several days later he thanked me for acting promptly. I also thanked him for sounding the alarm, letting me know something was wrong. His main fuse had blown, cutting out everything: engines, steering gear, and—after the alarm—the air for the whistle. I forgot all about the tea, and after docking, in the skipper's cabin, he insisted I join him in taking something stronger. I didn't need much coaxing.

It was early in the morning of January 26, 1933, still dark, with a strong easterly wind and sea, that the American Diamond Lines "Black Diamond" steamship *Black Gull*, Captain Trisco, lay hove to waiting to discharge Pilot Hugh McIntyre, 47, of Jersey City, off Ambrose light vessel. The pilot boat *Sandy Hook*, with Mate Harold Gjerloff and Pilot H.F. Miller on watch, rounded to under the ship's lee and dropped her yawl. It was manned by Apprentices Charles Peterson, 29, of Brooklyn, and Albert

Strandberg, 25, of Port Richmond, Staten Island. The ship had left Pier K, Weehawken, at 2:20 A.M., and it was snowing. McIntyre went over the side and down the ladder into the yawl and pulled away from the ship, which proceeded.

It was impossible for the *Sandy Hook* to lay under the ship's lee, so she made a round turn to recover the yawl. The yawl light disappeared, and the *Sandy Hook*, using her searchlight, searched desperately, working back and forth, with no result. The pilot boat *New York*, on Bar Station, and the U.S. Coast Guard were notified that the yawl and its three men were missing.

It has never been established, as far as I know, why, if the yawl light was out and wouldn't function, they didn't use the carbide water light lashed under the thwart or burn blue lights, which were carried in a canvas bag for just such an occasion.

Hours later, at 9:45 A.M., John H. Hubend was driving his bakery truck along Ocean Boulevard, Monmouth Beach, and saw the yawl a few hundred yards off the beach, having heavy going in the surf. Two men were rowing while the third steered. As he watched, an enormous sea struck the yawl and she went over. Hubend called the Monmouth Beach Coast Guard Station, and when Captain Carroll Osborne and eight men arrived the yawl was on the beach, upside down. A pair of oars and a life preserver were nearby. Coast Guard surfboats were launched and looked for the men, but they could not be found. The Sandy Hook Pilot Association notified their families. A double beach patrol continued to watch for the bodies. Peterson's body was never recovered. McIntyre's body was recovered and buried in Moravian Cemetery, Staten Island. Strandberg's body was recovered and, in his honor, a bell was installed in Wasa Lutheran Church, Port Richmond, Staten Island.

It was early in the morning of August 16, 1933, that I

boarded the new 880-foot Italian steamship *Rex* at Ambrose light vessel. Arriving on the bridge, I shook hands with Captain Tarrabotts, a tall, good-looking man with a full set of whiskers, and congratulated him on establishing a new transatlantic record. He looked amazed and asked, "How

The Italian liner *Rex* passes the Statue of Liberty on her way in to the North River piers. Edward Winters piloted her in on her record-setting "Blue Riband" passage in 1933. The 880-foot *Rex* was launched at Genoa, Italy, in 1931 and continued in transatlantic service between Genoa and New York until World War II. Laid up in Italy, she was bombed and sunk in 1944. Morris Rosenfeld photo. (1984.187.15921, © Mystic Seaport, Rosenfeld Collection)

did you know?" I then handed him several evening newspapers of the previous day, which gave various details of the records and also the *Rex*'s progress.

He thanked me, and with eager officers gathering around us he asked me if I knew the *Bremen*'s record. I replied 28.02 knots. With that bedlam broke loose, the officers hugging and kissing each other and patting one another on the back, for they had just gotten their own figure: 28.92 knots. They had crossed 3,181 miles of ocean, from Gibraltar to New York, in four days, 13 hours, 58 minutes.

It was a beautiful day, and as we proceeded to our pier we were given a salute and three whistles by every launch, tug, ferry, and steamer. Courtesy required us to answer each salute, but there was such a tremendous din that I instructed them to answer every third one, to give our ears a rest. We finally docked at Pier 86, North River, where the skipper presented me with a bottle and an autographed log of the trip. He was a fine man.

It was a lazy summer afternoon when I boarded the American four-masted schooner *Hesper* at Scotland light vessel, fanning along with all sails set before a light southerly breeze. The captain, a "downeaster," told me he was bound to Perth Amboy and his draft was 21 feet, 6 inches. He was in from Paraguana, Venezuela, with 1,800 tons of fertilizer and, as usual with sailing vessels, was short of food and water. I offered him a dozen cooked lobsters, which I had brought with me. He refused them with thanks, pointing to a pile of four dozen uncooked lobsters behind the wheelbox. I asked him where he got them and he told me that while becalmed off the New Jersey coast be swapped four bottles of rum for them from a lobsterman (this was during Prohibition).

We sailed in until the wind flopped. Then we anchored off the Hook, awaiting a tug which later towed us in to anchor off the Perth Amboy Dry Dock. On the way in the skipper asked me if I were acquainted with his cargo, and I told him no. He lifted up the corner of the hatch and told me to put my hand down. I did and found it quite hot. He told me that a Yankee gentleman traveling in Paraguana saw the people of the villages, where each family had a herd of goats, carting goat droppings to the outskirts of the town and dumping them. Over a period of years this became a small mountain, mixed with soil blown by the northeast trade winds. He recognized that this would make an ideal fertilizer ingredient.

This Yank inquired about the hill and was informed it was his for the asking; they were glad to get rid of it. He tested it, and later one part in 10 went into various patent fertilizers. He hired schooners to carry this stuff and cleaned up in more ways than one. In looking into the hold I expected to see licorice-type "jelly beans," but instead I saw a dark, rich brownish soil.

The only water on board was what he had caught in buckets and sails during a rain squall several days before, and it tasted awful, both in the raw state and in tea or coffee. After about 20 hours aboard, the tug landed me in Staten Island Shipbuilding Company (SISCO) Shipyard, and was I glad to guzzle some good cool water from one of the taps. We all take water for granted and waste it, but this experience made me appreciate it so much more.

On February 9, 1934, New York City had a record cold of 14.3 degrees below zero. The following night I had the steamship *Mauretania* out from Pier 54, North River. She sailed at midnight, going on a southern cruise to the West Indies. Some of her pipes and lavatories were frozen, and the paint was coming off her superstructure in large pieces. It was a clear, cold night, with a northwest wind and heavy ice running. Numerous buoys were out of position, and buoys 3, 5, and 7 of Ambrose Channel had lost their lights by being dragged under. Arriving at sea, I had to proceed offshore of Ambrose light vessel in order to find a clear enough space to be taken off by yawl.

Captain Peel told me he arrived the day before, experiencing a temperature drop of 84 degrees in eight hours. He explained he was in the Gulf Stream, 200 miles from Ambrose light vessel, doing 25 knots, with a temperature of 70 degrees. Eight hours later, he arrived at Ambrose, where the temperature was 14.3 degrees below zero.

On April 21, 1934, I had the American Hawaiian Line steamship *Ohioan*, Captain Reed, to sea from Pier 6, Bush Docks. This being a federal job, I was bound back light and took passage on the motor yacht *Alva*. I met the owner, W.K. Vanderbilt, and his wife (nee Warburton), a most charming lady, both very democratic. I worked my passage up and through the East River to Poorhouse Flats, just above the 23rd Street Landing. Here, after thanking the commodore, I was landed by the ship's launch.

Eight years later, on November 2, 1942, I took this fine vessel from the Bethlehem Shipyard, 56th Street, Brooklyn,

William K. Vanderbilt II had the 264-foot diesel-powered yacht *Alva* built in Germany by Krupp. He took her on a round-the-world cruise in 1931-32. As a passenger, Edward Winters helped pilot her through the East River in 1934, and in 1942 he piloted her when she was serving as the USS *Plymouth*. She was sunk in the Solomon Islands in 1943. Note her launches and a seaplane stowed aft. Morris Rosenfeld photo, 1934. (1984.187.69600F, © Mystic Seaport, Rosenfeld Collection)

to Pier 9, Staten Island. She had been renamed USS *Plymouth*, PG-57. She was torpedoed and sunk during the U.S army invasion of Munda, New Georgia, Solomon Islands, August 5, 1943.

June 4, 1934, was sunny and warm. Captain Ericsson of the tug *Margaret Olsen* had picked me up at Pier 6, East River, and was proceeding to the steamship *Alssund*, which was sailing at noon from Pier 36, East River. I was standing outside the wheelhouse talking to the skipper as we approached the Brooklyn Bridge, about midriver.

I happened to turn my head and saw something hit the water off our starboard bow, close by, with a huge splash. My first thought was that a packing case had fallen off the bridge, but suddenly I saw a body rebound out of the water, splash around a bit, then fall still. We drew alongside a young man, and the deckhand, cook, and I managed to drag him aboard. He was unconscious and limp, bleeding from ears and nose, but still breathing. We landed at the Fulton Landing Fire Dock under the bridge in Brooklyn and summoned an ambulance. His name was Goldberg, and in a despondent mood he had decided on suicide by jumping off the Brooklyn Bridge. Both his ankles were broken, and he had other injuries, but miraculously he lived.

On January 8, 1935, I was assigned to the Furness Line steamship *Queen of Bermuda*, lying at Pier 95, North River, bound to Bermuda. I went aboard and met Captain Davis, a most able skipper. This was the second day of dense fog, with in- and outbound vessels anchored all over the bay. Captain Davis decided to delay the sailing, and I stayed aboard overnight, the fog still dense. In the morning visibility improved slightly, and with a flood tide we decided to sail.

The Queen lay with her starboard side to Pier 95, with the Swedish steamship *Drottningholm* in the same slip, lying on the south of Pier 96. There was scarcely room enough between the two vessels for a tug, and we would have to come out "on the button" in order to clear the other ship.

Captain Davis sent word over to the *Drottningholm* to secure well, as we were about to sail. He also sent word to his engine room, telling them to open her up when he rang for "Full Speed Astern." I stood on the port wing of the bridge, looking down on the *Drottningholm* and wondering how we would clear her.

Very calmly, Captain Davis lit a cigarette, stood amidships, and gave the order "Let go all." When he got the "All clear," he ordered, "Full back all." They certainly did give her full astern down below. By checking landmarks it was clear that we backed out straight and did not set up much, but the other ship seemed much closer and then disappeared under our bow.

Out in the river, all clear, I saw what had happened. Both vessels drew about 26 feet, and there wasn't any more than 30 feet of water depth in the slip. The force of our rapid departure sucked the water after us and pulled the *Drottningholm* right away from the pier, breaking her lines and leaving her gangway hanging overboard. Prompt action by her crew in letting go of her anchors prevented her from following us into the river. This was the greatest demonstration of suction I ever saw.

In midriver and heading down, we could just make out the pier we had left. I walked over to Captain Davis, still amidships, and asked him if he knew what happened. He very calmly flicked the ashes from his cigarette and said, "Oh, that's alright, Pilot. The tug will take care of everything."

Mr. Andrew Anderson was a splendid pilot and a fine gentleman of Swedish decent, and when he died at the age of 70, May 7, 1935, his passing was mourned by all of his shipmates. June 2, 1935, was a beautiful day, and I was at sea on the pilot boat *Sandy Hook*. After dinner I went into her spacious wheelhouse, and after awhile I noticed a canister about the size of a gallon can on the radiator, which was about three feet in diameter and located in the middle of the wheelhouse. I asked the mate on watch what was in the canister and received the astonishing reply, "Mr. Anderson, Sir."

My first thought was to put this fellow in his place for trying to be funny, but he soon cleared up the mystery by telling me Mr. Anderson had left a request to be cremated and his remains to be buried at sea. Fortunately, on board we had Jim Berry and Frank Wall, close Masonic friends of Mr. Anderson, and after a little urging Frank agreed to conduct a brief service.

We all gathered on the quarterdeck, and we scattered the ashes and bones to the four winds and overboard with a little sermon. The location was about one mile south-southeast of Gedney Whistling Buoy, the area where he had spent much of his life, and his soul probably still stands watch, helping ships in and out of the harbor.

Pilot David Peterson was buried at sea in a similar manner. At the time of Mr. Anderson's burial there was no Bible available, so Frank had to compose his own sermon and did very well. After that, Mr. William E. Halliday, our president, saw to it that each pilot boat was provided with a Bible.

On December 21, 1935, I was assigned to the steamship *American Importer*, lying at Pier 60, North River, and sailing after midnight. I went to the pier, which was almost deserted except for a watchman, and boarded the ship. Here I met Captain Anderson, a swell guy. In his cabin he introduced me to Mr. Basil Harris, managing vice president, and we three had conversation until the ship sailed.

The night was clear, and we had a pleasant trip down the bay. The pilot boat *New York* took me out and landed me about 8:00 A.M. I was home only a short time when the phone rang. It was a reporter for the *New York Herald Tribune*, who asked me if I piloted the *American Importer* to sea. I replied that I had, and he then asked if Charles Lindbergh was aboard. When I said that I did not know, he replied, "You certainly would have known if he was aboard," and I then said, "Certainly not." A *Journal American* reporter also phoned, his conversation following the same pattern. I wondered what this was all about, and that evening the story broke.

Lindbergh, who had been hounded to exhaustion by reporters over the murder of his little boy, decided to sail to England for a rest. Arrangements were made with the

United States Lines, everything being "hush-hush," accounting for the presence of Basil Harris at sailing time. It was so hush-hush that the skipper did not even take me into his confidence; nothing was mentioned to me. I knew nothing of Lindbergh's presence. The reporters had gotten a tip, and they got my name and address with the consequent developments. I was pleased that he had eluded these reporter hounds and photographers, whom I had seen in action on ships on various occasions. They never rated very high with me in their actions, although they were only doing their job.

On September 3, 1936, I brought the British freighter *Langleecrag* in from sea to Quarantine. She was loaded with paper from Quebec and Three Rivers, Canada. Captain Brown invited me to his room and for about an hour related a most interesting story.

Earlier in the year, he was "tramping" in the Far East and was somewhere in the Philippine Sea when he received a typhoon warning. He got out his pilot guide to get information about the nearest safe harbor and, finding it, ran for it.

He came to anchor, glad to get shelter, and was immediately boarded by Japanese officers and an armed guard. He was not aware that this was a "barred area," and his pilot book, being a bit old, did not indicate this. They immediately sealed his radio, searched the ship from stem to stern, and examined the captain's safe and all his letters and papers.

He demanded that he be permitted to contact his government; this was denied. He was kept under arrest and surveillance in his room for two days. Then he was taken ashore and given a room with two armed guards outside his door around the clock. Then he was brought to trial and questioned incessantly for several days, defended by a government-appointed lawyer. Finally, after a week, he was permitted to sail.

The skipper, in telling this story, emphasized that the Japanese were up to no good, and that in his opinion were fortifying numerous islands as jumping-off bases if and when the "Big War" started. Japan was already at war with China since 1933, with the "Big War" still to come. I have often thought of this skipper and how prophetic his words and warnings turned out to be.

In the afternoon of December 9, 1936, Pilot George H. Seeth went aboard an "A&P" (American Pioneer) Line ship lying at Pier 58, North River. The Seaman's Union, Congress of Industrial Organizations (CIO) was on strike, so the ship's sailing was postponed until the following morning. George left the ship, walked off the pier, and crossed West Street, when a stranger engaged him in conversation. George's back was to the gutter, and the next thing he knew, he found himself in the hospital.

He had been blackjacked five or six times about the head and face, and when I visited him he had two beautiful shiners in addition to bumps and swellings. It was figured out that the stranger was a union decoy, who got George with his back to the curb and held him in conversation until a squad of goons came along in a car. They blackjacked George, hauled him into the car and worked him over, then dumped him with his bag in the gutter several blocks away. He hadn't been robbed.

Henry Clark and Harry Arnold, our New Jersey and New York Pilot Association presidents, went right to the bat with the CIO, accusing their goons of the dirty work, which of course they denied. They offered our men protection if we made a contribution to their welfare fund. Our men took a firm stand and refused, going instead to the police for protection. At first the police were reluctant, and we threatened to go to the governor. Our lawyer held that it was the Police Department's responsibility and that the city was liable in the event of any injuries. So we finally received a police escort to and from the piers.

Every pilot received a printed copy of police precinct locations and telephone numbers. A pilot receiving an assignment would call the precinct nearest to the pier, and they would pick him up at the nearest subway or elevated station and drive him to the pier through scowling picket lines. On having a ship in from sea, the reverse happened, the police driving the pilot to the nearest subway or el station from the pier. This continued for quite awhile with no further injuries.

We were all affiliated with the Master, Mates and Pilots, American Federation of Labor Local 22, and we were sympathetic to the seaman's cause. I held a card from 1916 to 1948 in Long Island 22. In our position as state pilots we never had occasion to strike; in fact, we wouldn't dare.

In the days of yellow fever and bubonic plague, all ships, large and small, arriving from a foreign port were compelled to stop at Quarantine off Staten Island for inspection. If the doctor found all well, the ship was given "pratique"—clearance—to continue. Immigration was heavy from the Mediterranean, and occasionally a ship had sickness aboard, necessitating detention up to 21 days at Quarantine. After a certain period, suspect cases were removed to the hospital on Hoffman Island, below the Narrows, and those dying were removed to nearby Swinburne Island and cremated.

I can remember Pilot Jimmy Cochran being stuck aboard the steamship *Italia* loaded with Italian immigrants. By law no vessel or boat was permitted to go alongside a quarantined vessel, which displayed the yellow Q signal flag. We received permission to send over our yawl and get him clean clothes and newspapers. He stayed aboard the full time.

Captain Tommy Taylor and Captain Crawford were on the Quarantine boats, and reporters Seguine and Dick Lee used to come off with the doctor's boat and board the ship after pratique was granted for news stories. Bo Nelson sometimes went off in a Whitehall boat to ships for news. Doctors Linton, Scott, Hudson, and Shields were boarding men before World War II, when they gave way to pharmacist mates, who did the boarding and examining.

Whenever there was a big arrival, such as Sunday night or Monday morning, it took quite some maneuvering and jockeying to get an anchorage, especially during flood tide. When you got a "horse" such as the *Berengaria*, on the flood tide with 20 vessels ahead of you, your work was cut out for you with plenty of eyes watching you and maybe helping you around with some "body English." To overcome the congestion and delays attendant to this situation, radio pratique was established on February 1, 1937. Under this system, any ship inbound with a doctor aboard could radio in that his ship was in good health and request pratique. The Quarantine Station would then grant pratique and the ship could proceed directly to her pier without stopping— however, a ship on her maiden voyage to this country was still required to make a Quarantine stop. This worked out wonderful and saved time and worry.

With the end of regular Quarantine stops, the taking of mail from incoming liners at Quarantine was discontinued on April 16, 1937. There were two mail boats, the *President* and the *John E. Moore*. As medicine progressed and immigration decreased, the Public Health Quarantine Stations on Hoffman and Swinburne Islands were abolished. During World War II, Swinburne Island served as a degaussing check center and Hoffman as a U.S. Merchant Marine training center barracks.

This system had been in effect for some time when the German steamship *Albert Ballin* requested and received radio pratique. Captain Lehmann, master of the ship, declared his ship healthy. The ship docked at Pier 84, North River, where it was discovered by authorities that there were several cases of typhoid aboard. Many of the passengers had already landed and eventually had to be traced and checked. The ship was penalized by being denied pratique via radio in the future in any American port, and radio pratique was denied on any ship commanded by Captain Lehmann—proper punishment for a man without honor.

On a nice day in the 1930s, Pilot Robert F. McRoberts, a boyhood neighbor and playmate of mine, took the motor vessel *Vistula*, a twin-screw tanker drawing 28 feet six inches, to circumnavigate Staten Island. The ship was loaded with water to make this test run. She left her anchorage off Stapleton one hour before the time of low water at Sandy Hook, passed through the Kill Van Kull, then down the twisting Arthur Kill and around the southern end of Staten Island to return to her anchorage. Bob modestly declined to take any credit for this feat, but it was the first time that a ship of that draft ever did it.

Captain Gilroy, port captain for Standard Oil of New Jersey, sponsored this trip to prove that the ship could navigate in narrow waters safely while loaded. The Baytown Pilots had refused to handle her because she was a bad actor. A number of our pilots said it couldn't be done, but Bob did it. The skipper was Captain Melguard.

It was a nice summer day before World War II, and Pilot Seabrook Wells was aboard the motor vessel *Gripsholm*, lying at Pier 97, North River, due to sail at noon. The skipper told him there would be a delay as a lady with a baby was flying in from Cleveland, trying to make the ship. Her husband was aboard and had intended to sail alone to see his mother in Sweden. His wife changed her mind and decided to go with him.

In order to avoid an extended delay, it was decided to have her land at LaGuardia, transfer to a seaplane, and meet the ship at sea. The ship sailed and proceeded to sea,

Edward Winters (left) pilots the Norwegian training ship *Christian Radich* during her visit to New York in 1939. (Courtesy William G. Nagen)

to rendezvous with the plane. The skipper had ordered a boat cleared for the transfer, and the pilot suggested that the pilot boat yawl be used. He thought it a good idea. They reached Pilot Station at the appointed time and did not have long to wait before the plane landed close by the ship and pilot boat. A yawl was launched by the pilot boat, went alongside the plane, took off the lady and youngster along with their baggage, and ferried them safely across to the ship, which had a side port opened. The pilot then went down the ladder into the yawl and over to the pilot boat. With a three-whistle salute and thank you, the ship proceeded.

It was March 16, 1939, and we were just getting over a lousy southeaster, with fog and rain. Visibility was improving, and the wind was working around to the west, with a

A long climb on a good ladder: a Sandy Hook Pilot boards a steamship in February 1937. Morris Rosenfeld photo. (1984.187.78290F, © Mystic Seaport, Rosenfeld Collection)

continuing southeast swell, when the loaded tanker *Garnet Hulings* came along, just east of the Whistler.

She lay almost before the swell and had a ladder at her port side, a short climb. We pulled alongside and, as the yawl rode up on a swell, I reached for the ladder, got my foot on a rung, and promptly found myself overboard. Apprentice John Ackerman grabbed me over the stern, and I tried to get back into the yawl, but with my overcoat and oilskins on I found this impossible. Finally rising up on a swell, I grabbed the ladder and climbed aboard. The ladder was a good one, with flat rungs nicely varnished, but slippery.

The mate, who was at the ladder, waited for and took my bag. I went up to the bridge, where I met cheerful Captain Ericsson, who shook my hand and said, "What do you say, Pilot, full speed? She's on slow speed ahead now."

I thought, "Gee, what a skipper; he sees me fall overboard and doesn't even mention it." We put her on "Full" Ahead just as the mate came up with my bag.

Seeing the situation, he said, "Captain, did you know the pilot fell overboard?"

"My God, no," he said. "I saw the yawl come alongside from the window of the bridge, then went into the wheelhouse to put her slow ahead. Mr. Mate, take the pilot below and see that he gets some dry clothes."

The mate took me into his room and said, "Gosh, Pilot, you're a big man; what size collar do you take?"

I said, "Size 18, waist 44, shoes 10 1/2."

He was about five foot six, wore a 15 collar, had a 34 waist, wore a 9 shoe. I stripped and dried, then put on a freshly laundered pair of khaki pants—was able to button three buttons on the fly—put on a lamb-trimmed jacket—was able to button one button. I put on a pair of overshoes without socks—could just get into them—no underwear, shoes, or shirt. I went to the bridge and proceeded to Quarantine, the sun shining brightly, wind west, and a beautiful day. We anchored and the boarding officer came aboard, and later I went below to the saloon where they were checking papers and crew.

I figured I would have some fun with old Doc Shields, Curry the Customs officer, and Hoffman the Immigration officer. I went to the table where Doc was working and said, "How are you, Doc?"

He glanced up, then down, then up, and adjusting his glasses, said, "My God, man, where did you get that rig; I didn't know you." I told him, and he said, "Have you chills? Had a stimulant?" The old Doc liked his stimulant, and I think he was a bit disappointed when I told him the ship was bone dry, but that I had had some coffee. So we all had more coffee.

After awhile the mate came in and said, "Pilot, if you will come to my room, your clothes are dry." I was surprised that in a short two hours they should be ready, but they had been dried in the fire room and dried fast there. It was like getting into a coat of armor, with everything stiff, and getting into my shoes was torture; they seemed two sizes smaller.

The mate had been so kind, I said, "Mr. Mate, here are a couple of bucks for yourself or the boys who dried my clothes."

He said, "Pilot, you are very kind. Thanks, but I wouldn't think of taking it."

I replied, "Thank you very much, Mr. Mate, for what you have done for me, and I hope that if ever you fall overboard I'm around so I can return the favor and do the same for you, even though my clothes will fit you loosely." Needless to say, I was glad to get home and, after a bath, get into something comfortable.

On August 22, 1939 I boarded the West Coast lumber ship *Pennsylvania*, loaded with lumber. Day was breaking as we proceeded in. The skipper was violently outspoken against unions, and in our conversation he gave numerous logical reasons.

After we anchored off Stapleton, he offered me a room to get a few hours sleep. I declined his offer with thanks, telling him a boatman would shortly be off to take me to shore. He turned in, and while I stayed on the bridge the radio officer approached me and invited me into his shack, just above the wheelhouse. I accepted, went in, and sat down.

He said, "Pilot, I was listening to what the captain said, and I don't like it." I soon discovered that he was an ardent Red and most eager to shove the "Red line" down my throat. What he didn't know was that I had been hoping to meet one of his kind and to find out what really makes him tick. Well, here he was and soon we were at it "hammer and tongs." He said he was as good as any capitalist, and "Henry Ford—he sits on his fanny, rolls up the millions through and by the sweat of the worker's brow; what good is he?"

I disagreed, saying, "Maybe you are as good as Henry Ford, but I don't think I am by a long shot. As I see it, Henry Ford through his pioneering, ability, and hard work created an organization that produces a car at a price that the masses can afford, and in so doing, creates work for a million workers. I manage to hire a housekeeper or someone to mow my lawn; that is about as far as I go in creating work for my fellow man. What actually do you do for your fellow man? All you and your fellow Reds do is to tear down, rip to shreds, anyone who is successful. By the way, why are you in this country anyway? This country which gives you free speech, freedom of opportunity and religion, equality before the law, freedom to work where you choose.

In Red Russia any remark or criticism of the government makes you an enemy of the State, subject to being shot, or worse, sent to Siberia. You work where you are told; they fix the wage rates. You cannot travel from town to town without police permission, and if you do not play ball with the commisars, your food card might be revoked, you starve or are sent to work in the mines, where you die within three years.

"You vote for only one slate of candidates (who must all be members of the party) during so-called elections and God help you if you don't vote, or register a write-in candidate. If Red Russia and what it stands for is so wonderful, why aren't you there? Why don't you and your fellow Reds take the next boat to the Red Paradise and enjoy real Russian freedom?

"Do you know what a Red is? Well he's a guy who has nothing and is willing to share it with you."

"Oh," he said, "that's an old one, and mark my words, before many years, the unions of this country—the workers will run this country. We have 15,000,000 members now, and every worker will be forced to join."

This continued back and forth for some time, and suddenly he said, "Pilot, I think you would be a good Communist."

I agreed, saying, "You are right. When the day ever comes when the Commies can give me anything better than we now have such as freedom of speech, religion, to choose a job, travel—unencumbered—then and only then can you count me in."

The man on watch announced the Stapleton boatman alongside. I went down, and as I was leaving, Katzmann gave me *The Communist* and a copy of the New Constitution which contained, among others, this gem: "From each according to his ability, to each according to his needs."

On the night of March 13, 1940, I got aboard the motor vessel *Tamerlane* at Ambrose light vessel. She was a 17-knot Wilhelmsen ship loaded with manganese ore from Africa. We proceeded in, and on the way the captain told me that, although the draft was 28 feet 11 inches, she was very tender, so I should not give her too much helm, unless necessary. As we rounded buoy 10, Ambrose Channel, with an easy right helm, she rolled violently, and I knew then what the skipper meant. We anchored in Quarantine, and after a nightcap I was shown to my room, off the saloon.

The passengers—about 10 men—were sitting around tables with numerous bottles and glasses, enjoying their last night aboard. I turned in, and it wasn't long before all was quiet and I feel asleep. Some time later I was awakened by smashing glasses and bottles, and I almost rolled out of my bunk. I do not know the degree of the ship's roll, but it was sufficient to clear the tables of their glassware. The mate on watch told me later that it was the turn of the tide when a fast Esso tanker passed, hooked up, bound to sea, and her swell caused the roll. He also told me that the ship's tenderness was due in part to the fact that most of their fuel was used up. But in all my life I never experienced anything like this; namely, a 10,000-ton freighter loaded down to 28 feet 11 inches rolling glasses and bottles off the tables while anchored in Quarantine.

It was December 24, 1940, Christmas Eve, and I wasn't in a very happy frame of mind. Two men had knocked off in the office, giving me the last turn in the Sea Company and the Norwegian sugar tramp *Norne* to take to sea from Pier 33, Brooklyn, at 8:00 P.M.

I went aboard and gloom was evident everywhere, mixed with some inebriation. I met the skipper; then, having time kill, was invited in to the mate's room. The mate had tears in his eyes as he asked me to join him in a drink. He remarked how rough it was, with everyone ashore going home to have a nice Christmas Eve, here they were sailing for Cuba, not knowing if their families in Norway were dead or alive, Hitler and his beasts having taken over their country. I felt a lump in my throat as he handed me a photo of his wife and two children from his dresser. I realized that I was a pretty lucky guy compared to these good Norwegians.

Suddenly there was a knock on the door and, upon opening it, there stood Captain Skrogen, who was to take the ship from the dock. He was a big and good-natured Bay Ridge Norwegian, and he asked the mate to send some men ashore to pick up some packages. Surprised, the mate told Captain Skrogen that they had everything aboard and were ready to sail.

The packages came aboard, and at Captain Skrogen's suggestion the crew was mustered on deck. There, every man aboard the *Norne* received one package as a Christmas gift. The gloom was instantly transformed into joy and smiles as the men opened their packages, which contained knitted sweaters, socks, caps, gloves, or vests. How wonderful it was not to be forgotten. Captain Skrogen received the sincere thanks of every member of the crew for the organization that made this event possible, namely the Scandinavian Ladies of Bay Ridge (Oslo Heights). They had worked all year, knitting and sewing, so that every man on a Scandinavian ship at dock or anchor in the Port of New York, would not be forgotten on Christmas Eve. Surely, each and every one of these good ladies had a Merry Christmas knowing how theirs gifts were received and appreciated.

I had the watch after midnight, January 8, 1941, aboard the station boat *New York*, with a fresh northeast wind, white caps, cold and clear. The Waterman Line steamship *Josephine Lawrence* came out of Ambrose Channel, passed inshore of us, and headed down for Scotland light vessel. She had no pilot. When she got down there, she started shooting parachute flares and notified us that she had lost a man overboard somewhere between Ambrose Channel buoy 7 and Scotland light vessel. We at once steamed in, retracing her course, put men on lookout, swept the area with our searchlights, and sent up flares. We did this for about two hours without result, at which point the ship thanked us and proceeded. I had never used this type of flare before and each one lit up a considerable area for quite a period of time.

It was July 18, 1941, that I boarded the steamship *President Johnson*, lying at Pier 9, Jersey City, to sail at 7:00 P.M. This was the old four-masted, single-funnel steamer *Manchuria*, built at Camden in 1904. She was deep loaded on a draft of 35 feet. We were delayed and sailed the following morning. The skipper, Captain Ehmann, said that this was the deepest that the ship had ever been and wondered how she would steer. She was a bit sluggish on the first helm, but did quite well until we got down to Ambrose Channel buoy 5. We were doing 12 knots and gave her left helm to break a sheer to starboard. Breaking the sheer, we steadied the helm, but she kept swinging to port. A loaded tanker was coming in on our port bow, and we had to stop the starboard engine and back it full to clear her, which luckily we did.

Once clear of the tanker, we had to reverse our engine, movements, and rudder to keep from going ashore. By this time we were outside the Channel Entrance with plenty of room to maneuver. The steering gear was then tested and found to be OK. The skipper investigated, but up to the time I left him had not solved the mystery. Had someone shut off the steam while we were on the left swing, so we couldn't steady up? Whether by accident or design, we both agreed it should be reported as possible sabotage. When I got ashore, I reported the details to Captain Bayliss, U.S.C.G. He requested that we report all similar incidents.

On August 4, 1941, I took the Dutch motor vessel *Tosari* from Pier 3, Bush Docks, to Gravesend Bay Explosive Anchorage, where we loaded about 750 cases of explosives. This took several hours, and after lunch I had a most interesting talk with Mr. Woltjers, who on April 22, 1941, had escaped by small boat from Holland to England in spite of the Nazi patrols.

He was the son of a professor and was bound to Sourabaya, Java. After we finished loading, we hove up and proceeded to sea, where I left the ship after shaking Captain VanDenderen's hand and wishing him good luck and a safe voyage.

Several months later, November 11, 1941, I received a phone call from Bill Hanley on Pier 3, Bush Docks, telling me he had a small package for me from Captain VanDenderen. I asked him to send it over, and to my great surprise it was a tobacco pouch I had left on his ship when she had sailed from New York in August.

The skipper had found it after I left, taken care of it, and in Sourabaya had taken the trouble to place it aboard a British Silver Line motor vessel bound to New York. I thought this was the height of thoughtfulness and consideration, sending this one-dollar pouch around the globe to restore it to its rightful owner. I immediately sent a letter of appreciation and thanks.

Chapter Five

"It's a Hurry Up Job"
Piloting during World War II, 1941-1945

For many years prior to World War II, we could look for two or three ships to arrive from the Near East sometime early in August, loaded with dates. It was on August 4, 1939, that I boarded one of three ships, the German motor vessel *Reichenfels* at Ambrose light vessel, bound for Quarantine and 33rd Street, Brooklyn.

Arriving on the bridge, I was greeted by a pleasant German skipper, to whom I gave some newspapers and magazines. On the front page of one of these, *The Daily News*, was a full-page picture of Nazi Storm Troopers giving a Jewish storekeeper a going-over with a rifle butt, after smashing his plateglass window across which had been splashed, in white paint, a six-pointed star and the word "Jude."

In conversation, I found the skipper to be quite broad-minded and used to American habits and customs. He had sailed the Great Lakes for five years on another German ship, the steamship *Tractor*, which carried autos. We anchored at Quarantine, and two of the ship's officers, having been passed by the doctor, came into the chartroom and started looking at the newspapers I had brought aboard. These men were much different from the mild skipper, being regular Nazis, arrogant with a chip on their shoulders. One of them, seeing the picture on the front

Chapter Five

._A._A   Give Call Letters
__O.E   Give Call Letters Secret Identity
___..Z...S   Give 3 letter hoist—Pilot Number
___O_.N   Stop
._..L_.N._T   Proceed
.._I_.N._T   Give secret identity (Navy)
_.__Y__..Z..._X   Suspect

SIGNAL TOWERS, 1942-6

Barge Office
U 41
Statue
U 42
Starrett 26th St. N.Y.
U 43
Seamen's Institute
U 44
D. L. & W. R.R. Hobo ken
U 45
Pier 6 Bush Docks
U 46
Borough Hall S.I.
U 47
Ft. Wadsworth
U 52
Any Tower Call
U 40

page of the *News*, said to the other in German, "Verdamte lugen" (damned lie) and a variety of slurs and comments about our country, also spewing out his hatred for the Jews. I understood every word, but held my tongue until he turned to me with fire in his eyes, blurting out in broken English, "Hitler wants not krieg" and other baloney. I figured it was about time to shut this guy up, and I felt ready for him, for I had listened to Hitler's rabble-rousing broadcasts and also those of club-foot Goebbels, which they kept dinning into the ears of the German people: "Ich will bein krieg"—I want no war—until the people actually believed him, meanwhile preparing day and night.

I said to this second officer, "Ich spreche deutsch"—I speak German—and also told him I had overheard and understood everything that he had said.

He seemed surprised and a bit flustered, and in the ensuing verbal battle I was able to throw into his teeth facts and figures I remembered from Hitler's and Goebbels's speeches. These two madmen repeated over and over, "I want no war."

"The international Jew and Jewish bankers," I told him, was just so much nonsense. At the same time, they were drilling and arming, boasting of their planes and subs, etc. The officers could not refute any of my statements based on Nazi speeches.

The Quarantine officers left, the skipper came on the bridge, and while proceeding to the pier he had coffee and cake served. He was a distinct moderate, and I thought he knew war was coming. As you know, World War II started in three weeks—September 1, 1939—with the "Blitz Krieg."

World War II began in Europe in September 1939, and the German subs got busy at once, sinking the Donaldson liner *Athenia*. On March 29, 1940, the Halifax pilot boat was torpedoed; 9 lives were lost.

On July 12, 1940, the steamship *Gypsum Prince* was sunk by a mine. Our old friend, Captain O'Shea died after two days in a lifeboat.

All Japanese ships entering and leaving New York were under U.S. Coast Guard escort, in and out. My first ship under these conditions was the motor vessel *Yamikawa Maru*[1] in January 1938.

On June 1, 1941, the new green buoy marking the anti-submarine net off Hoffman Island was established. The navy also mined areas at Craven Shoal and Swash and began mine-sweeping off Sandy Hook. On August 25th gas rationing went into effect. After Pearl Harbor on December 7th, we had our first air-raid alarm on December 9th. On December 20th the gate in the antisubmarine net was narrowed, and all American ships were painted gray.

On September 10, 1941, the steamship *Steel Seafarer*, Captain Halliday, was bombed and sunk in the Red Sea. Albert Beggs, Pilot Sam Beggs's son, and all hands saved.

January 2, 1942, tire rationing in effect.

January 8th, the Eastern Steamship Line steamship *Cornish* was established as a guard boat at the Whistler. The Scotland, Fire Island, and Barnegat light vessels were replaced by buoys. All ships were ordered to observe blackout at sea.

January 14th, the steamship *Norne* was sunk 60 miles west of Nantucket, 39 lives saved.

January 15th, the tanker *Coimbra* was torpedoed and sunk off Southampton, Long Island.

January 16th, only entrance and turning buoys in Ambrose Channel lit. Convoys starting through Hell Gate, Long Island Sound, and Cape Cod Canal.

January 19, 1942, the Grace Line steamship *Santa Elisa* arrived in a sinking condition under tow after a collision at sea. Pilot William K. Wood, who boarded the vessel, pro-

1 This vessel has not been identified. Winters may be referring to *Yamakaze Maru* or the *Yamahuzi Maru*.

Chapter Five

ANTISUBMARINE GATE SIGNALS

Out
East Gate . _ _ W .
West Gate _ . . . B .

In
East Gate _ . . . B . plus _ 1 long
West Gate   . _ _
W . plus _ 1 long

Two- way
Alternating in & out signals
every 1 minute

Closed
East Gate
Code Flag O.D.
Baker at Mast

West Gate
Code Flag W.Z.
Baker at Mast

Closed at Night Anchor Lights -
Fog - Ringing Bell

CONVOY DESIGNATIONS

HX : Halifax
Gus : Gibraltar— US
GN : "Gitmo," Guantanamo North
UK : United Kingdom
ON : Overseas North
ONF : Overseas North, Fast

ceeded up Ambrose Channel until the ship grounded in the channel between buoy 13 and 15. Her draft was 57 feet. She floated on a rising tide and finally was beached at Lower Bay Ridge Flats.

February 14th, I had the last coastwise Clyde Line boat, *Norfolk*, Captain Dexter, outbound to Charleston, Jacksonville, and Miami.

March 19th, Pilot Richard J. Bigley was on the U.S. destroyer *Stringham* as it depth-charged a German sub south of Ambrose light vessel. The U.S. Army Corps of Engineer dredges no longer dumped at sea, but in the Narrows. The mud tows upriver now and dump under the Washington Bridge.

In April we started using Pier 18, Staten Island. Barracks were being built along the Staten Island docks. The navy's new subchasers were on the job. On April 6th, the steamship *San Jacinto* (ex-Mallory liner) was torpedoed and shelled by a German U-boat. Our old friend Captain Hart was killed. On April 17th, Claremont and Mariner's Harbor Docks were completed, and the large pier and munitions depot was completed at Earle, Leonardo, New Jersey.

April 26th, the U.S. Coast Guard takes the pilot boat, *New York*, which is designated CG-1902.

April 30th, the Long Island lights are reduced and the New Jersey shore is blacked out.

Pilot Joseph Seabrook Wells boarded the Norwegian motor vessel *Reinholt* at Ambrose light vessel. She was loaded with coffee and had been shelled in battling a German U-boat 60 miles south of Ambrose. She escaped with minor damages. Pilot J.S. Wells retired January 19, 1943, a swell shipmate.

It was in May 1942 that Pilot Gustav Swainson took the old British freighter *Audacieux* from Craven Point with orders to anchor in the Explosive Anchorage, Gravesend

The pilot boat *New York* was taken over by the U.S. Coast Guard in April 1942. Repainted battleship gray, she was designated as the Coast Guard Reserve vessel CGR-1902 from June 1942 to November 1945.

Bay. For some reason, probably engine trouble, Gus anchored this "HOT" ship off Staten Island. The Coast Guard officials fell around Gus's neck and suspended him on the 15th. Gus, a good and very conscientious pilot, dropped dead on the 19th, his death induced probably by worry over this incident. He lived in a beautiful home in Garden City with his wife, Margaret (Schwall), and one son, Gustav, who graduated from Annapolis, July 14, 1944, with honors. His dad owned the lobster schooner *Mary and Emma*.

May 1st, food registration in force.

May 8th, during the first five months of World War II, the Allies lost 178 ships on the coast.

It was midnight, May 10, 1942, when I left Pier 18 with four other pilots on our launch to board ships anchored off Staten Island. These ships were part of a 42-ship convoy sailing on the early morning tide. After putting these men aboard their ships, we continued to look for my assignment, the motor vessel *Talisman*. After three hours we gave up the search and returned to Pier 18. I went to the office, looked in the Club for a bunk—all were occupied—so I lay down on a long table in the office. About one hour later Bill Huus, who was on duty, called me, telling me a bunk was available in the Club, so I went there and corked off, being dead tired. About 7:00 A.M. Bill woke me, saying, "Mr. Winters, I have a job for you. It's a hurry up job—the *Queen Mary*. They are all ready to sail, just waiting for the pilot."

Still in a daze, I thought, "Is this guy kidding? Anyway, I am still attached to the motor vessel *Talisman*." I soon realized that this was an emergency and I had better get to Pier 90 pronto. I got a cab, told him to step on it, which he did, and we reached the pier in jig time. Here Captain McConkey met and escorted me to the single gangway still out. The *Queen* was still singled up, Captain Herb Miller and his tugs all ready. Captain Snow on the bridge met me, remarking about the good time I had made. I cautiously approached the question whether a pilot had been ordered the night before. I was assured it was no fault of the Pilot Association. I dropped the subject and had the distinct feeling that this was a hush-hush sailing. She was loaded with about 15,000 troops and we proceeded to sea, bringing up on the tail end of the freighter convoy. The weather was clear and fine. Arriving outside and leaving the bridge, I shook hands with the skipper, who had made out my orders as "steamship Monster."

I started down for the side port, and it took about 12 minutes, with officers as an escort, to fight our way through the troops, clogging passageways. This situation was corrected in the subsequent sailings by having the passageways cleared for the discharge of the pilot. It was important to discharge the pilot with the least possible delay and keep the vessel moving, so as not to be a sitting duck for German U-boats, which were working close to New York Harbor.

The *Queen Mary* had a draft of 40 feet 10 inches, length of 1,018 feet, and beam of 118 feet 7 inches. She established a transatlantic record in August 1938: Ambrose to Bishop's Rock in three days, 20 hours, 11 minutes, averaging 31.69 knots.

The Cunard liner *Queen Mary* entered New York Harbor for the first time in 1936. The 1,018-foot ship, driven by four screws powered by steam turbines, made the first commercial transatlantic crossing in less than four days. As a liner she could carry as many as 2,332 passengers; as a troopship during World War II she could carry more than six times that many soldiers. In this 1936 view, she lies in Quarantine off Staten Island, with the "doctor's" boat alongside for pratique. Morris Rosenfeld photo. (1984.187.74963F, © Mystic Seaport, Rosenfeld Collection)

The *Queen Mary* and *Queen Elizabeth* carried 15,000 troops apiece—a total of 1,500,000 during World War II. Built at Clydebank, Scotland, by John Brown & Co., the 81,237-ton *Queen Mary* had 160,000 horsepower and burned 1,100 tons of fuel per day at 28.5 knots. She was equipped with two gyroscopically controlled stabilizing fins on each side.

This ship arrived at New York on June 1, 1936, on her maiden voyage, with Pilot W.K. Wood. Captain Fred Muller of the Quarantine boat took Mrs. Gibson, Jenkins, Marian, and me around the ship anchored at Quarantine for a "look see." I piloted her in on December 14, 1945, on a draft of 37 feet 10 inches, when she was commanded by Captain Fall.

May 13th, the new explosives anchorage was established at the Statue, marked with green buoys 29-31. I got unlimited class X gas card.

May 26th, the Stapleton boat service is at Pier 24, Staten Island.

May 29th, I had the steamship *Henry S. Grove*, Captain Graham, to sea. This was my first commodore ship.

June 13th, we sent 51 men to sea, including Amboy and vacation men.

June 15th, a convoy of 27 ships came along at twilight, beautiful. By this date, 315 vessels had been sunk since January 1st.

June 16th, we now run ships over the new degaussing range off Swinburne Island.

The American steamship *Pipestone County* had been torpedoed and sunk, and the survivors were rescued by the Norwegian motor vessel *Tropic Star*, a small 10-knot freighter. They reached a spot about 200 miles off Boston with the weather calm and clear, and a smooth, glassy sea, when the lookout on the port wing of the bridge sung out,

"Stick coming up out of the water on port bow, close aboard!"

The skipper rushed out of the wheelhouse, ordering the helm hard over, and sure enough, there about 400 feet away was a U-boat starting to surface. Approaching at a 45-degree angle, heading for the ship's port side, he passed under the ship, counter grazing the rudder. The sub then submerged. The ship's crew, assisted by the *Pipestone County's* gun crew at the "Ready," watched and saw her surface about 1,000 yards away. Miraculously, the ship's gun crew scored a hit with the first shot at the U-boat and were credited with a kill. There were no survivors.

I had a full day on this vessel, June 22, 1942, when the skipper told me this story. We left Pier K, Weehawken, early in the morning and had two runs over the degaussing range, adjusting compasses with "D.G." on and off. Then we went back to Gravesend for "ammo," finally anchoring off Staten Island to await a convoy.

On November 10, 1939, this good ship had picked up survivors of the Booth Lines steamship *Clement* ("Para boat") sunk by the German raider *Graf Spee* off South America.

June 26th, a navy and cargo convoy arrives at 10:30 P.M., some sight.

June 28th, eight German saboteurs landed by U-boat on Long Island with $170,000. Saboteurs were also landed in Florida, but all were captured.

July 1st, I had the steamship *Argentina* #4, Captain Simmons, out. Taken out by U.S. Navy launch, Lt. Wood. I was landed at Pier 7, East River, and had a conference with Capt. Reinecke.

July 4th, a convoy of 21 arrives at 8:00 P.M. I had the steamship *Andrea F. Luckenbach*.

July 20th, the gate in the net closed suddenly, with 10

ships coming in before the tide. One patrol boat was sunk.

July 26th, two ships collided in the East River, bound through Hell Gate, Pilots Brakke and Fordham—Hot?—Lucky.

August 1st, U.S. Army takes Staten Island and Bush Docks. We start on board with Jerseymen.

August 6th, the first convoy out from the new Army Base, Staten Island. I had the steamship *Uruguay*, Captain Spaulding.

August 21st, I took out war-risk insurance: $1.00 per $1,000—$10.80.

August 31st, Marian, Bill, and I drove to the Highlands. With visibility unlimited, we saw a convoy arriving ahead of time. Beat it to the office.

Sept. 7th, we had first real air raid alarm at 2:30 A.M., requiring blacked-out lights on cars.

September 8th, over 40 ships arrived in fog.

September 9th, USS *Wakefield* (ex-*Manhattan*), Captain Bradbury, burned at sea. It was towed in to Boston, with 1,600 transferred at sea. Chief Engineer Kaiser.

September 10th, a convoy of 35 ships sailed. I had the Russian steamship *Alma Ata*, Captain Feodorov.

September 12th, three convoys arrive, 70 ships, with visibility unlimited. The first ship arrived at Quarantine, followed by ships half a mile apart to the horizon, about 15 miles away. Some sight.

September 16th, pilot boat *Wanderer* put 30 men aboard ships anchored in North River for 97-ship convoy. Ships were anchored from the Battery to above Yonkers.

September 18th, I had the steamship *Pan-New York*, Captain Thompson, out. Vice Commodore Weems on board. Fog, easterly winds. Our three motorboats were out of commission. Using picketboats.

It was about 3:00 A.M., September 19, 1942, and I was

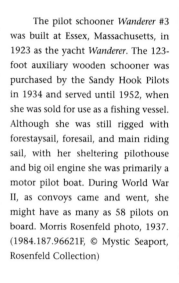

The pilot schooner *Wanderer* #3 was built at Essex, Massachusetts, in 1923 as the yacht *Wanderer*. The 123-foot auxiliary wooden schooner was purchased by the Sandy Hook Pilots in 1934 and served until 1952, when she was sold for use as a fishing vessel. Although she was still rigged with forestaysail, foresail, and main riding sail, with her sheltering pilothouse and big oil engine she was primarily a motor pilot boat. During World War II, as convoys came and went, she might have as many as 58 pilots on board. Morris Rosenfeld photo, 1937. (1984.187.96621F, © Mystic Seaport, Rosenfeld Collection)

turned in on the pilot boat *New Jersey*. I was awakened by voices and men moving about. I looked into the alleyway and saw men wet and in their shorts, wearing Mae Wests, coming aboard. My first thought was that some vessel had been torpedoed. Such was not the case, however. These men, 34 of them, were the crew of the armed trawler *Pentland Firth*, preceding a convoy and running without lights, that had been struck by U.S. Mine Sweeper 81, also running without lights and sunk. These men boarded the

New Jersey, then were transferred to the pilot boat *New York*, taken up and landed. Later that day I had the motor vessel *Rena*, the commodore ship of a 22-ship convoy, in.

September 21st, the Cunard steamship *Aquitania* sailed from Pier 17, Staten Island, on a draft of 36 feet six inches, with Pilot W.S. Ireland. This was the largest ship to occupy these piers.

October 27th, coffee rationed, canned goods scarce. Aquarium being torn down.

November 1st, I had the steamship *Utahan* out in 44-ship convoy. With thick, intermittent fog, we anchored four times.

On November 4, 1942, I was put aboard the Panamanian steamship *Kotor*, along with two U.S. Coast Guardsmen armed with .45s. She was an ex-Latvian about 40 years old, not very big and with none of the comforts of home. She was anchored off 160th Street, North River, along with many other anchored vessels awaiting a convoy. Pilots weren't in Coast Guard uniform yet, and armed guards accompanied us on all neutral vessels in and out. We had a special room for them on the *New Jersey*.

Most of them were nice young men with little training. I went to the captain, reported, checked his pass out, hoist anchor, and while talking the two guards barged in and joined in the conversation. A short time later, I went to the ship's small and dingy saloon and talked to the mate, an old-timer. After awhile the guards barged in again and, uninvited, joined in the conversation. One of them said, "Say, Mate, how can you ever sail on an old tub like this?" By this time I was quite angry and diverted the mate out of the room by rechecking hoist.

Later on, I returned to the saloon and gave the guards a lesson in behavior. I told them whenever they boarded a vessel to consider it as home for its crew and show respect accordingly. "Always knock on a door before entering any-one's quarters. Don't look down on a crew member because he is a foreigner or ill-dressed. I have met some highly edu-cated and intelligent men who didn't look the part. Don't ever belittle a man's ship, no matter how lousy she may appear. Remember you are only aboard for about eight hours, but these men are aboard day in, day out, gale, fog, subs, bombers notwithstanding. Only rugged men can take this, not griping weaklings. All foreigners show respect for authority, and as U.S. Coast Guard representatives you boys have a duty to perform in carrying out your orders. As rep-resentatives of the U.S. government, you must carry your-selves with dignity to earn that respect and give our coun-try a good name." There was more, and later the guards thanked me for setting them straight. I am sure they were better men after my lecture. I have found, in all my years as pilot, that courtesy and consideration pay handsome divi-dends.

November 5th, our new launch *Ambrose* cost $28,000— not so good.

November 13th, Bill Hagen joined the pilot boat *New Jersey* and got a Coast Guard uniform.

It was the night of November 13, 1942, that I dropped out on our motorboat *Lillian B.* to board the steamship *Robin Goodfellow*, just inside Ambrose light vessel. It was clear, with the wind west, blowing a gale. The ship drew 26 feet eight inches and had a lee on her starboard side. Just as we drew alongside, a line (which we didn't need or want) was dropped over the side of the ship and trailed aft under our bottom. Suddenly, the line got into our propeller, swinging us around. The ship, with a little headway on, towed us stern first. We were taking seas over the stern; what a mess.

Billy Mitchell and Jimmy Canvin did heroic work, with

Chapter Five

The Sandy Hook Pilots became part of the U.S. Coast Guard Temporary Reserve in November 1942. This group in their Coast Guard uniforms, sitting in the well-appointed mess room of the pilot boat *New Jersey* (2), includes Warren Sullivan, Andrew Oldmixon, Bill Hagen (third from right), John Roche, and Allen Peters.

seas lapping over the stern, in freeing the line, and I don't know to this day how they did it. It took about 10 hectic minutes and I finally made the ladder. After making sure that the motorboat was maneuverable, I took the ship in to anchor at Pier 23, Staten Island, and the next morning to Erie Basin.

November 14th, Mayor LaGuardia, Captain Reinecke, and General Drum took a trip on CG-1903 (*New Jersey*) to observe dim-out.

November 23rd, both the New York and the New Jersey Pilot Associations joined up with the U.S. Coast Guard Temporary Reserve (R)(T).

December 1st, I had the Brazilian steamship *Midosi* in at night. With the wind northeast and heavy seas, we steered from aft. She was one of 44 ships arriving.

December 2nd, Hilton Lowe chose me to go up North River to help convoy get underway. On tug *Grace Dalzell* in a southwest gale, blowing 75 mph, freezing.

December 7th, invasion barges sailed. They were 157 feet long, made 18 to 22 knots, had 25 crew, carried 250 troops.

December 8th, Captain Wardlaw made provisional pilot; quits on the 20th.

December 9th, steak costs $3.20 for 3-3/4 lbs. WOW!

December 11th, "Black Friday," I had the steamship *Lena Luckenbach* (ex-Eastern *Soldier*) built in Japan in 1920. On this foggy day, 107 ships sailed. I was on the job for 22 hours.

December 14th, Hilton Lowe and Edgar Anderson inducted into the U.S. Coast Guard (R)(T).

1943

January 1st, had motor vessel *Bowenville* in. Commodore Woodward.

January 3rd, Marian took forty chocolate bars, stamps from Ed to British Routing Office in care of Commodore Woodward for Captain Matheson's family in England.

January 6th, I had British steamship *Ruahine* out. Was Pilot on her in World War I

January 7, Sworn in to U.S.C.G. (R)(T) #45665, Pilot No.17.

On January 27, 1943, I brought the 488-foot tanker *Stanvac Manila* in to anchor at Quarantine, just inside the Narrows, her assigned berth. She was Commodore Ship— Commodore McCabe, Captain Dahl in command. She drew 31 feet. At 11 P.M. the following night after a northeast snow and sleet storm I was ordered to Stapleton Landing, Pier 24 S.I. to board a SOCONY tug and shift this vessel, which had dragged. I met Port Captain Vander Heuvel and we boarded the tug and proceeded to the ship.

There were no motorboats running, and I wore my uniform for the first time. The ship had two anchors down and had dragged well below the Narrows, through the Cable Area. New Captain Karlsen thought he had the cables; so did I and expected a mess. We hove in the port anchor with 45 fathom of chain and were relieved when the mate announced, "All Clear." We then hove in 90 fathom on the starboard anchor, in fear and trembling awaited the result. Strange to say, that anchor came up clear also. How do you explain it; a ship drags through a cable area with two anchors down and doesn't catch a cable? A mystery to me. We finally anchored safely back in Quarantine, blowing hard, clear and cold out of the north. What a job I had to keep my new uniform cap on my head.

February 1st, Pilotage on ships in transit cut 50%.

February 4th, I had steamship *Loriga*, Capt. Newlands in. First time in dense fog thru Net. Whistler moved 1000 yards 110 degrees.

February 5th, I had motor tanker *Preventor*, British Captain Morrison, triple screw, from 42 N.R. towing old World War I wooden ship, *Birchwood*, loaded with wood pulp, bound to Camden, N.J. I made up the tow, towing alongside thru Net. Passed 20 incoming ships on ebb tide. Coast Pilot Brinkman, a former towboat man, gave me good advice, how to make tow fast.

February 6th, attended conference in Port Director's Office after being assigned to Commodore Ship, *Tivives*, Captain Peterson, Commodore Fisher.

February 12th, Outside Guard Boat moved North and West.

February 13th, French cruiser *Richelieu* arrives—Pilot C. Gallagher.

February 15th, I shifted motor vessel *Carrillo* fouled by Liberty Ship—8 degrees below zero.

February 16th, Motorboat *Sandy Hook* ices up—sinks—raised—Lost January 5, 1944.

February 20th, I shifted steamship *Perseus*, Captain Rundel, motor vessel *Garonne*, steamship *Nailsea Court*,

The Sandy Hook Pilots began to use motorboats during World War II, as the volume of convoy traffic exceeded the ability of oar-powered yawls to deliver and take off pilots efficiently. Here, the motorboat *Pilot* comes alongside with a group of pilots and apprentices in their Coast Guard uniforms.

Captain Lee, services on motor vessel *Trondhjem*—very cold.

February 27th, U.S. Navy Barge put me aboard steamship *Gloucester* from Pier 11, East River. Ships Battery to Yonkers—86 ships sail.

March 1st, our (N.J.) Agent Dave Little dies. Swell Guy.

March 5th, I had a full day on the destroyer HMS *Chelsea*, Captain Wilford, adjusting compasses, degaussing on and off—calibrating direction finder, ran degaussing range, gun practice, hedge-hog firing.

March 8th, we are now Assistant Examination Officers for ships.

March 14th, had steamship *Umvuma* British Commodore Ship—85 ships out.

March 18th, had Dutch steamship *Stad Vlaardingen*, adjusted compass off Craven Shoal with weak tug *W.F. Dalzell* assisting. Navy Ensigns McBride and Jenkins did the job. On strong ebb tide, tug could not push us around so we drifted thru the 600 feet. Gate sideways. The ship was

480 feet long. The mate on the bow was waving for us to go astern, the second mate on the stern for us to go ahead—humorous.

March 19th, steamship *San Simeon* anchored in North River, drags, hits 3 ships, sinks off Guttenberg.

March 23rd, had Swedish motor vessel *Svealand*, Captain Anderson out. Commodore ship.

March 29th, meat rationing in effect

April 1st, steamship *Wm. D. Pender* out—back in fast picket boat then steamship *Horace Binney* to anchor, to sea, fog, rain. We have 10 men in Hell Gate.

April 12th Pilot Leon Oldmixon had USS Battleship *Iowa* on her trials.

April 19th, boarded 33 ships at night with yawls—wind N.E. strong, rain, heavy sea.

On April 24, 1943 the former Morgan steamship *El*

Though largely replaced by the motorboats, pilot yawls continued to be used, especially when conditions were too dangerous for a motorboat. Here, John Madigan and Clem Corson, dressed in Coast Guard fatigues, prepare to set off in a yawl, perhaps to visit the nearby light vessel, dressed in her wartime gray paint. Note the wire span with lifting ring that was used for hoisting the yawl over the rail of the pilot boat. The 14-foot sweep oars and the heavy wooden tholes in which they were rowed show clearly in this photo.

Estero, loaded with munitions at Craven Point, caught fire. The burning vessel was towed away from her berth to a point off Robbins Reef and scuttled. Here she lay with her decks awash. Captain Ole Ericksen of Olsens was in charge of the operation, using 2 Olsen tugs alongside, the tugs *Beatrice Bush* and a Band O tug ahead. The ship was raised, September 14, 1943, towed 200 miles to sea and sunk. It was rumored that in addition to being "hot" she also had ingredients for bacteriological warfare aboard. The U.S. Coast Guard assisted. On December 16, 1944 Captain Ericksen and all crew members who participated in this heroic episode received medals, which they richly deserved.

April 28th, to sea HMS *477*—British LST 316 feet long, had 2 tugs on deck, 133 CBs aboard—73 sailed.

April 29th, had USS *Monticello* 371—ex-*Conte Grande*, out. Captain Coyer, Commodore Ship of largest troop convoy to leave port. Special.

May 7th, had steamship *Bernard N. Baker* to sea. Has new anti-sub streamers.

May 12th, had USS *Simpson* out. Old 4-piped destroyer. 14 1/2-knot convoy.

May 22nd, had motor vessel *Empire Viscount*, ex-*Athelviscount* in. Torpedoed last year, repaired.

May 28th, had William A. Richardson out. 78 ships, mostly Liberties.

It was on a beautiful day, May 31, 1943 that I was assigned to USS *Iowa*, BB-61, lying in Gravesend Bay, bound to sea, draft 36 feet 6 inches. Our motorboat put me aboard for a 7:00 P.M. sailing. It was still daylight and she was laying to the East of the flood tide heading, almost through the Gate. I met Captain McCrae, (President Roosevelt's aide at Casablanca) and Executive Officer Cassaday, who told me there would be a delay in sailing to about 11:00 P.M.

This was due to the fact that Harry Hopkins and his baggage would be late.

His presence was strictly, "hush-hush" and while we waited, we swung to the ebb tide. Finally, everything was ready and we proceeded to the bridge and conning tower. This I was told was 20-inches-thick steel and enclosed the wheel, telegraphs, and other instruments. We stood on the small bridge surrounding the tower and the captain told me to use the phone in giving steering directions to the quartermaster at the wheel, rather than through a 3-inch slit, his only view ahead. This seemed odd to me at first, standing only about 6 feet from him; he inside, me outside the conning tower and I soon found out it was the most practical thing to do. We got underweigh and the skipper informed me he would turn the ship and for me to aid him.

The battleship *Iowa* (BB-61) was built at the New York Navy Yard and commissioned in February 1943. Here she prepares to move from Bayonne to Gravesend Bay late in March 1943. Edward Winters piloted the 887-foot ship to sea in May 1943, after which she served in both the Atlantic and the Pacific during World War II. (NH 53264, courtesy Naval Historical Center, Washington, DC)

I told him it was strong ebb tide and it would be best to proceed to the Narrows to turn. I asked him how she handled and he answered, "Like a tug."

We proceeded up to Red Buoy 20A below Fort Hamilton and put the helm hard left, the skipper saying, "Watch her swing, Pilot." Swing she did, but also forged ahead, so I cautioned him to back the port engines, stop the starboard. He thereupon turned the ship over to me, much to my relief. I didn't like being an advisor. We backed up once, then straightened out, down through the Gate in the Net. She steered and handled beautifully. She was almost 900 feet long and showed no lights, except for small running light and side lights—way inboard. If you made her head on, you could easily take these lights as belonging to a trawler. I shall never forget the respect shown me by these fine men and how orders given were executed.

Everything ran like clock-work and made me proud of our Navy and its men.

June 10th, motorboat *Gem* catches fire, taking me to steamship *Magister* at night. Leaking badly—some ride—Lucky.

June 15th, had steamship *Atlantian* out. Back on pilot boat *Wanderer*, then to sea on same, largest day in Pilot history. Over 200 ships.

July 5th, RAF plane tows glider loaded with 1 1/2 tons across 3,600 miles.

July 12th, had steamship *Liberty Glo* out. Had this same ship just after World War I into Black Tom. She had broken in two then—put together again.

July 22nd, had motor vessel *Laurits Swenson*, Captain Rodin. Commodore Rear Admiral King retired R.N. Largest group to leave Great Britain—88 ships—66 for N.Y.—averaging 9.7 knots. No casualties—coffee rationing ends.

July 30th, handled 202 ships in and out Friday.

August 7th, steamship *Sam Houston II*, Captain Pena, out—steamship *Edwin M. Stanton*, Captain Hiers, in. Wind westerly, visibility unlimited. 90 out and in-coming ships.

73 in sight. Wonderful sight. A line of ships extending from Quarantine, seaward, out about a half mile apart, to over the horizon at sea.

August 21st, USS *Anne Arundel*, Captain Lewis, out with all black troops. Another contingent composed of all Japanese.

August 23rd, I passed (overtaking) Jack Lyons in the Gate with steamship *Baron Cawdor*. Had to write a letter of explanation.

September 2nd, had British tanker, *Iroquois*, Captain Collister, out. I piloted her in World War I with Captain Scott.

September 15th, USDE *Penniwell* commissioned at Brooklyn Navy Yard. George Neumiller, Chief Yeoman— Jane, President.

September 19th, had Swedish motor vessel *Svealand*, Captain Anderson, out. Commodore Ship, Commander Pillsbury, ex-Navy officer, USS *Raleigh*, ret.

September 30th, easterly gale at night; boarded convoy with yawls.

October 5th, had steamship *Henry Lomb* (hot) in Gravesend. Passed George on USS *Penniwell*, DE-175, out-bound.

October 8th, had US battleship *Arkansas*—Captain Richards to sea from Gravesend.

October 10th, had steamship *Gulfbelle* in, Commodore.

October 18th, had USS *Ariel* AF-22 (ex-*Jamaica*) in, Captain Hylant. Once ran thru a 100-mph hurricane off Mona Pass. Navigating Officer Biel explained radar to me. Wonderful.

October 23rd, two Gulf tanks, *Gulfbelle* and loaded Gulfland, collide off Florida—88 lost—plus my pipe which I left aboard *Gulfbelle* when I had her in on the 10th.

October 25th, mines around Net taken up—New

anchorage at Craven Shoal.

It was a stinker, rain, fog, heavy sea, and easterly winds up to 75 mph. I was one of the 40 pilots ordered to sea on the *Wanderer*. Due to the weather, the *New Jersey* ran in to Gravesend Bay, where we transferred, then proceeded to sea. The ETA (estimated time of arrival) was 2:00 P.M. for an O.N. (Overseas North) convoy. These were all flying light, in ballast, vessels and we were hoping the commodore would head offshore and await more favorable conditions. Such was not the case, however, for he made it "right on the button" and the fun started. With visibility one-half to one mile, the ships flying light "laying to" before an easterly gale and sea, we were constantly being driven in to leeward, our motorboats were getting a terrific banging, and our boys were doing heroic work.

Just as I got on the turn our motorboats gave up the ghost and had to run in; this meant using yawls. I was called for American Hawaiian steamship *Georgian*, Captain Vaughn, an old-timer. He had a good lee and ladder and I was standing by on the *New Jersey*'s upper deck with my bag ready near the pipe rail. I had taken my white shirt and black tie off so they would not get wet and put them in the bag. While rounding the ship's stern, the *New Jersey* took a terrific roll and I watched my bag—shirt and all—slide through the rail and overboard, winding up in Davey Jones's Locker. The ship had a good lee and ladder, was a big climb, rolled heavily, and I got aboard safely. Captain Vaughn was glad to get in and we finally anchored at Quarantine, with 90 fathoms of chain, with the second anchor ready to let go. We rang off the engines and the skipper invited me into his room.

I couldn't give him any newspapers or magazines, because they were in my bag, now reposing in Davey Jones's Locker, so I had to give him the news verbally.

When it came time to turn in, the skipper said, "Pilot, I want you to take my room and bed."

I said, "Skipper, I wouldn't think of it."

He said, "Pilot, you don't understand. Tonight I am going to be the Pilot and turn in the Pilot's room. You be the captain. I am dead tired, been on my feet 24 hours and need a good night's rest."

I said, "OK, and I hope you sleep well." He turned in and in no time was "deado."

I talked to the mate, had coffee, and later went on the bridge for a look around. It was the turn of the tide and we were head to a strong east wind, our stern clearing the upper end of Quarantine Dock by about 250 feet when stretched out to our 90 fathom of chain. Everything looked OK till I looked on our port side and there I made out in the glare of a cluster light, a ship's bow—two anchors down, dragging down, broadside to the wind, heading for us amidships. She was also setting in on the rocks above Quarantine. Ordered engines on standby, call the crew, heave away, and after what seemed ages, managed to touch the engines ahead, heaving up. The dragging vessel, the Liberty ship *George Dewey*, Frank Wall, Pilot, cleared us and wound up on the rocks. After shifting anchorage, I turned in.

In the morning we docked at Pier 4, Weehawken, and was I a mess, unshaven (my shaving gear went overboard in my bag), no shirt or tie and in uniform. I had to keep my coat collar buttoned up around my neck and felt very self-conscious traveling on the ferries and trains to the Office and home.

The pilot boat *New Jersey*'s stabilizer went out during the storm and she certainly took a pounding, as did the motorboats. Four ships of that convoy got ashore before they got pilots. The *F.J. Luckenbach* at Belmar, *Exilona* and *Fort*

Douglas at Sandy Hook (later got off), and a Liberty ship high and dry on the Hook. She was floated some weeks later, declared unfit for service, and used as a bombing target offshore.

Pilot Tom Torgerson had an American submarine to sea during a heavy easterly in World War II. Our motorboat tried to get alongside but could not do so safely. The captain invited Tom to come along for a trip down the coast to Norfolk. There wasn't much else he could do, so he said OK. Away they went, and after getting into deep water they ran quite smoothly, submerged a good part of the way.

1944

It was June 3, 1935, a beautiful day when the French steamship *Normandie* arrived on her maiden voyage with Richard J. Bigley as her pilot. She averaged 29.62 knots and cost $60,000,000 to build. She was turbo-electric drive, steered and handled well. At the captain's request, Dick Bigley had her out when she sailed on the 7th. She was 951 feet long, 117 feet beam, 39 feet draft, 82,799 gross tons. I had her out December 26, 1938.

We took her over in the early days of World War II, converting her into a troopship. It was on February 9, 1942, clear with a strong northwest wind, that she caught fire while lying at Pier 88, North River. The fire was started by a careless workman using an acetylene torch in an upper deck salon. In spite of the fire watch, the fire spread rapidly through the "donkey's breakfasts" (mattresses) which had been piled there for the troops. The shore fire companies arrived and poured thousands of tons of waters into her upper compartments and rooms, causing the ship to list. It was suggested to open the sea cocks and put the ship on the bottom. While debating this, she gradually turned

The 1,029-foot French liner *Normandie* made a grand sight entering the Narrows in 1935. This stylish ship held the Blue Riband for fastest transatlantic crossings several times after entering service in 1935. Edward Winters piloted her out in December 1938. The ship burned at her North River pier in February 1942 while being converted to a troopship. She was scrapped after the war. Morris Rosenfeld photo. (1984.187.71233F, © Mystic Seaport, Rosenfeld Collection)

over on her side into the slip.

After spending about $5,000,000 to right her, she was towed to the Naval Supply Depot, Bayonne, on November 3, 1943 by 20 tugs, Captain Herb Miller in charge. Here she was examined, and it was decided that she was not fit to be repaired.

On January 11, 1944 she was towed from Naval Supply Depot, Bayonne, to Columbia Street, Brooklyn, by a fleet of tugs. I witnessed this from the bridge of the Liberty ship I had just brought in from a convoy which had just arrived. Ships were anchored all over the Bay, and she wormed her way through, cut across the lower end of the Flats, up Bay Ridge Channel to Columbus Street.

I had expected her to fetch up on the lower Flats, which she didn't, and as she later passed close to me, I saw that she only drew 28 feet. This was nice work, I thought, on the part of the towboat men, but there was more to come.

On November 28, 1946 she was towed from Columbia

Street to Port Newark. This called for the utmost skill, organization, and teamwork. Gauging the tide, making the turn at Bergen Point, easing through the bridge, where the boat alongside had to let go and pick the ship up again after passing through, called for the highest type of skill—truly a remarkable job. Arriving at Port Newark, she was cut up for scrap.

January 16th, I had the steamship *Louis D. Brandeis*, hot, out from Craven Point with a full load of ammo, bound to Gravesend Bay. It was 5:00 A.M., still dark, clear, strong ebb tide, and the ship drew 27 feet 6 inches. After two McAllister tugs got us into the Channel, the tug skipper told me he had to get to Hell Gate in a hurry, so could not escort me to Gravesend. A Coast Guard rule provided that all "ammo" ships moving in the Harbor must have at least two tugs alongside. So the tugs left and we proceeded through the vessels anchored, and there, coming in through the Narrows, was the first ship of a 23-ship convoy. We reached Craven Shoal, but could not cross the incoming line of ships to get into Gravesend. So we passed through the Gate over the degaussing range, then dropped the anchor, backed and filled until we were head to the current. After the last ship of the inward convoy passed, we hove up and picked a berth among the eight other ships anchored there. Captain Badge and I were both relieved to be safely anchored.

January 20th, had motor vessel *Abraham Lincoln*, Captain Holman, Commodore Dunne. Record sailing.

January 21st, pilot boat *New York* back on the job.

The pilot boat *New Jersey*, was laying near the Whistler and breakfast time was approaching. The date was January 27, 1944, Charlie Britton was on watch and visibility was zero due to dense smog. Pilot Jack Dearstyne, several others and myself were in the smoking room, listening to radio

Chapter Five

The pilot motorboat *Command* (CGR-3097) lies alongside the pilot boat *6*. In the background is the pilot boat *New Jersey* (2)—CGR-1903. Launched at Bay City, Michigan, in 1929, as the motor yacht *Olive K.*, the 157-foot vessel was purchased by the Sandy Hook Pilots to replace the *Sandy Hook* in 1940. The *New Jersey* was damaged in a collision with the tanker *Fairfax* in January 1944, but was repaired and returned to service.

station WOR when we heard a steamer's horn, coming steadily closer, outbound. The radio announcer had just said, "and now the time is exactly 7:10 A.M. Eastern Standard time," when WHAM!! the outbound T2 light tanker *Fairfax* struck us plumb amidships, first striking the extended yawl crane. We rushed on deck, alarm bells ringing, and there we were, impaled on a huge towering bow of the tanker. We were riding up and down on it with the heavy southerly swell. A yawl was launched, some heroes leaped into it, while the rest of us tried to launch a lifeboat. I kept an eye on the electric lights, feeling that as long as we had them, the engine room wasn't flooded. The chief engineer made a survey and reported that we wouldn't sink, much to our relief. Coast Guard boats, later on, picked us up via radar and stood by.

The *New Jersey* was built for Mr. Kettering, inventor of the self-starter, as the *Olive K.* She had a nickel-steel hull, and a gyroscopic stabilizer, which in bad weather reduced her roll about 25 percent. She replaced the sunken *Sandy Hook* on February 24, 1940. After the collision she proceeded to dry dock for repairs.

January 28th, had motor vessel *Rangitata*, Captain Willand, Commodore Lox, to sea. Three Liberty ships break in two in O.N. Convoy

February 5th, Dutch motor vessel *Sunetta*, anchored off Stapleton discharges 56 20-mm antiaircraft shells, hitting Pilots Harold Kaiser's and George Kissenberth's homes—also others.

February 8th, had USS *Blessman* DEB-69 in. Captain Gillis, Executive Officer LaBoutillier, son of president of Pennsylvania R.R.

February 10th, had steamship *Esso Charleston*, Captain Bosch, out. Commodore Bunnell.

February 25th, received letter of thanks from Captain Milledge for 1-year issue of *National Geographic Magazine*.

March 15th, motor vessel *Gripsholm* arrives with exchange prisoners.

April 10th, steamship *El Coston* sunk at sea by T2 tanker *Murfreesboro*.

It was a fast U.K. convoy that T2 tanker *Murfreesboro* collided with ex-Morgan Liner *El Coston*, the latter sinking. This happened April 10, 1944 and the tanker returned to New York, arriving there on April 26, 1944. She was loaded with 87-octane gas and had a large hole in her port side. Amboy Pilot Charles F. Peters towed her in to Port Socony with the assistance of 6 tugs. With the damage of the fire and explosion ever present, all hands were glad to get tied up safely. Her draft was 31 feet 8 inches.

April 12th, steamship *James Woodrow*, Captain Plikat, out. Fog. 75 sailed.

April 13th, Ed at Camp Carson, 913th Infantry, PFC32690471—Colorado.

April 15th, used auxiliary Gate, first time in fog, on steamship *Juan Casiano*, inbound.

April 18th, US LST-*534*, Captain Blake, out. 98 ships sail.

April 26th, Pilot Charles Peters tows T2 *Murfreesboro*, with large hole in port side, leaking 87-octane gas, to Port Socony with 6 tugs—31 feet 8 inches draft.

April 14th, U-boat *550* destroyed 140 miles east of New York. Had sunk tanker *Pan Pennsylvania*.

May 11th, Danish steamship *Scandia*, ex-*F.D. Asche*, in. 60 depth charges on deck. Fog.

May 12th, USS cruiser *Marblehead* #12 out. Captain Kraker. Steering gear trouble.

May 19th, steamship *Ephraim W. Baughman* out. Captain Savicki. 107 ships.

May 21st, new steamship *Bulkcrude*, Captain Gross, in. Largest tanker in world [500 feet], 163,000 barrels, 100-octane.

May 28th, steamship *Frank A. Munsey*, Captain Stidham, Commodore.

It was on May 31, 1944 that I was on the bridge of the *Queen Mary*, lying at Pier 90, North River, along with Captain Bissett and Captain Herb Miller of Barrett Tugs. It was approaching sailing time, 9:00 A.M., first of the flood and dense fog.

We contacted the Gate Boat at the Net, also the Outside Guard Boat, and both reported visibility zero. The ship drew 41 feet two inches and was loaded with 15,000 troops. After waiting until 10:00 A.M., tide running strong, still dense, we agreed to postpone the sailing until the next low-water slack. This would be about 10 hours; it wasn't considered prudent or wise to sail on the ebb tide. Captain Bissett thanked us; we shook hands and left the ship. As Captain Miller and I walked down the pier together, we agreed that, along with Captain McConkey, we had made the right decision.

I returned to the office and was placed first on the

Board, the next assignment being for 12:30 P.M. Suddenly, several telephones rang: one was the Port Director's Office ordering a pilot for the *Queen* at once; the other was the Cunard Line asking if the pilot would take her out on a falling tide, it being high water slack. About 1:00 A.M. Ralph Ferd and Edgar Anderson spoke to me about using my own judgment and, with time being of the essence, I told him I would go to the ship at once and decide there. I hopped a cab and was whisked to the ship and aboard in jig time,

The *Queen Mary* comes up through the Narrows on her maiden voyage in 1936. Repainted gray as a troopship, she came into New York frequently during World War II. Even longer than the battleship *Iowa*, and with a 41-foot draft, she was the largest ship the Sandy Hook Pilots had to maneuver in the crowded harbor. Edward Winters piloted her in May 1942, May 1944, and November 1944. (1984.187.74963F ©Mystic Seaport, Rosenfeld Collection)

where I found everything ready. It had cleared, and I told Captain Bissett we would sail, which we did at high water slack. The captain was concerned about the draft of 41 feet and falling tide, but I assured him all would be OK if we went at a reduced speed, since the ship squatted another two feet at half speed.

Chapter Five

We proceeded without incident thru the Gate in the Net into Ambrose Channel, with a strong ebb tide, going "Slow" or "Dead Slow," but making the turn in Ambrose she hesitated and we had to stop the port engine. She straightened out down the last leg, steering well, and now it was almost low water. The captain suggested more speed, but I told him the tide was at its lowest, and we continued "Slow," getting out safely. The following day, Captain McConkey phoned, asking me about sailing the *Queen* on a falling tide, and what I thought. I said I wouldn't advise it. He agreed with me and told me the navy pushed the idea and, after we were reported out safely, called him up and said, "Well, she made it." The Cunard Line opposed sailing on a falling tide, but the navy pushed the idea and was willing to take the chance.

June 2nd, motor vessel *Peebles*, British Captain Nicolson, out. 9,000-ton economy vessel, burns 6.6 tons fuel per day at 9 knots.

The US CVE *Guadalcanal*, an escort carrier, was 487 feet long, 80 feet beam, and carried 1,500 in crew, 10,200 tons loaded, 18 knots. On June 4, 1944, this vessel under command of Captain Dan V. Gallery, captured U-boat *505*—150 miles off Cape Blanco, Africa. It was the first time the U.S. Navy had boarded and captured an enemy warship since the War of 1812. The sub was brought to New York, then towed up the St. Lawrence to Chicago, where it has a permanent home in the Jackson Park Museum.

June 6th, USS *DD-126* in to Pier 8. Captain Enos told me this was D Day. Gustav Swainson, son of Pilot Gus Swainson (dec), graduates from Annapolis.

July 8th, George Tompkins back from Cherbourg invasion. His ship, USS *Glennon*, sunk.

July 10th, had old Norwegian steamship *Bergensfjord*, Captain Velte, on full speed trial trip. 27th Street, Brooklyn, to sea via Swept Channel, 4 miles past Buoy ZED (Old Whistler) to 97 North River. Mr. Tribble adjusted compasses. 12 hours on the job.

July 17th, steamship *David Bushnell*, Captain Hunter, out. HOT. 110 ships in H.X. Convoy.

July 18th, had steamship *Robin Sherwood* out, Captain Bonn. Last trip bound west, light from England, developed 54 degree list. Returned to port safely. Ballast shifted.

July 21st, we have coordinators now on boats. Pilots— William Wood, Bert Donnelly, J.D. Baeszler, R.J. Bigley.

July 24th, steamship *William Black Yates* out, Captain

The 450-foot, steam turbine-powered freighter *Robin Sherwood* represented an efficient new American design when she entered service for the Seas Shipping Company in 1941. Here, before the U.S. entered World War II, she is painted with the national flag to announce her neutral status to German U-boats. Edward Winters piloted her in July 1944, during her North Atlantic convoy duty. Morris Rosenfeld photo. (1984.187.101661F, © Mystic Seaport, Rosenfeld Collection)

Rylander. 114 ships sailing.

August 3rd, had T2 tanker *Sappa Creek*, Captain Riddle, out. This vessel was anchored off 75th Street, North River, drew 32 feet, and was loaded with high-test gas. In getting underweigh windlass trouble developed. Finally, we were ready, about 3 hours late and Captain Weldon, aboard Port Directors' Tug, informed me to try to make the convoy, giving me a deadline of about 50 minutes to make the Gate. The skipper also wanted to make the convoy and as we proceeded down the river, we gave her "Full Ahead" whenever we could. Coming down toward the Battery, heavy traffic developed, causing us to put her on slow. We were bowling along pretty lively and nothing happened, the engine indicators showing a steady 87 revolutions. We were getting into a traffic jam and this situation called for action. We rang engines to "Stop"—but they continued. Called engine room, and we were informed by the engineer—"We can't slow now, we'll blow her up." Well, luckily, we bowled through the traffic about 15 knots, no doubt scaring everything out of our way. Upon investigation, we found that the engineer (probably new to the ship), upon getting "Full Ahead" opened her up, instead of keeping her on reduced harbor speed. This was my first T2 turbo-electric tanker and they handled swell, but required a 15-minute "Stand by" to reduce speed from "Full Ahead, sea speed," to "Harbor Full" or "Maneuvering." We made the convoy.

August 7th, Gravesend Bay dredging finished.

August 9th, had USS *Jicarilla*, towing 4 barges 7,000 miles to Pearl Harbor. Convoys split now, run alone. Subs almost finished.

August 20th, pharmacist mates replacing doctors at Quarantine.

August 26th, USS *McNulty*, DE-581, Captain Crafts. Navy Yard to Earle for ammo. Then to Buoy 6, Raritan Bay Channel, for calibration, then to sea. On the job 6:30 A.M. to 8:10 P.M.

September 2nd, motor vessel *Skotass* in to 82nd Street, North River. 102 men for convoy, including Dalzell captains Al Howell, Roy Coon—Hell Gate men, Mitchell Bohn, also our Amboy men. 105 ships in.

September 8th, had USS *Bronstein*, DE-189, Captain

Kinney, Navy Yard to Earle to sea. She had sank 5 subs.

September 9th, had Swedish steamship *Ivan Gorthon* out. Painted in peacetime colors.

September 14th, hurricane winds southeast to northeast 70-90 mph—north 99 mph. Fog—rain.

September 22nd, steamship *Pierre Marquette*, Captain Hoffman, 27 years old, in. First trip.

September 23rd, Pilot Hilton Lowe made captain.

October 9th, steamship *Lucien B. Maxwell* in. Made 8 round trips to Utah and Omaha Beach. Heads in Normandy from England.

It was 2:00 A.M. October 14, 1944 that I got a hurry call to proceed to Pier 10, Staten Island. Here I boarded DE-231, *Hodges*, bound to sea ahead of a convoy. It was thick fog and ebb tide with ships anchored all over the Harbor. The skipper told me had radar (which I had never used before), and coming down between the vessels, anchored off Staten Island, it was almost useless. We cleared the Narrows, shaped down for Craven Shoal, which we located via radar. We never saw it and continuing thru the Gate, then Ambrose, made the buoys via radar without seeing them.

This was new and most interesting, and as we passed buoy 1 we heard another destroyer in the Upper Bay, over the intercom, tell that he was about to anchor, it being too thick to proceed. He had no pilot. I was trying to make the Guard Boat, when suddenly I heard an anchor chain rattle and let go. It sounded right under the bow, and I was on the verge of stopping the engines when I realized it was the destroyer anchoring off 69th Street in the Upper Bay. Pilot George Seeth bound out ahead of me in another DE heard the same thing and did stop his engines. What a wonderful age we are coming into—spotting or locating buoys without seeing them and hearing a vessel anchoring 10 miles away.

October 28th, USS *Wakefield* (ex-*Manhattan*), Captain Raney, in. Commander Jack Dempsey aboard. She had 5,000 "Kraut" (German) prisoners. Had apprentices Turnrure and O'Donnell along for a passage. They had some job getting ashore at Pier 51, North River.

November 3rd, had steamship *Queen Mary* out, almost low water, draft 41 feet 2 inches. Capt. Bissett.

November 6th, Captain Gorrett, British compass adjuster, drowns in Long Island Sound.

November 7th, four Liberties loading ammo at Leonardo (Earle).

November 15th, USS *John Ericsson* (ex-*Kingsholm*), Captain Anderson, to sea with troops. Commodore Tillman.

November 21st, steamship *Irwin Russell*, Captain Platzer, in to anchor on Flats. Steamship *Pachaug* struck us on port side at engine room, flooding it. Beached.

It was November 27, 1944 that I had motor tanker *Lucellum* in from sea, and on the way in we had several close shaves, but Captain Swenson never batted an eye. After anchoring at Quarantine for the night he invited me in to his room for a night cap and chat. I gave him newspapers and magazines, for which he was genuinely grateful; magazines being practically nonexistent in England. In the course of the conversation I mentioned how calm and collected he was in an emergency, and he said, "Pilot, I have been running high-test gas ever since the war started about 5 years. I can remember my first trip—I had my clothes on all the way over and laid down occasionally on a locker in the chart room. The second trip I did better; I laid down in my bunk on occasion and so on, until now, after squaring away in convoy, I put on my pajamas and have a good night's rest in my bunk. You see, I have good reliable officers."

He then told me how, loaded with 8,000 tons of high-test gas, in convoy, following the coast of England, a German bomber strafed them with four bombs, one striking just forward of the engine room; another blew an anchor out of the hawsepipe. She was immediately transformed into a "Bunsen Burner," necessitating the cutting away, rather than the launching of lifeboats, most of the crew getting away safely. An escort A.S.R. equipped with foamite went alongside and, after using tons of the extinguishers, smothered the fire. This was done with a loss of about 700 tons of the precious gasoline. The ship was towed to Manchester, repaired, and put back in service.

In the beginning of World War II, tanks reaching England would discharge their cargo of high-test gas and immediately sail back in convoy. When a torpedo struck one of these tankers, they were blown to bits due to the remaining gas in their holds. New orders were issued, and all tankers after discharging, were "gas freed" and inspected before sailing. Numerous tankers were subsequently torpedoed, but made port.

December 3rd, motor vessel *Comanchee*, Captain Bourke, in. Commodore Griswold.

December 11th, to sea on pilot boat *Wanderer* with 30 men. Easterly gale, rain. Great difficulty boarding U.C. Convoy. What a night!!!

December 16th, Captain Ole Ericksen and crews of two Olsen Tugs, one B&O tug, and tug *Beatrice Bush* get medals for towing ammo ship *El Estero*, afire from Caven Point. Scuttled at Robbins Reef.

December 23rd, steamship *Thomas W. Gregory*, Captain Schaeffer, in. Held ship off Pier 19, East River, from 10:30 A.M. until 5:00 P.M. when Moran docked us.

December 28th, steamship *Alexander W. Doniphan*, Captain Sharpe, in with 900 tons of mail from France.

1945

January 2nd, small tanker *Sunoco* blows up off Leonardo. 11 lost.

January 4th, USS *Mirth* #265, Captain Rusteen, in to Leonardo, discharged ammo, then to Marine Basin, Gravesend Bay. First time for me.

January 10th, 800 ships—70 miles long, land at Lingaen Bay—110 miles from Manila.

January 23rd, steamship *Joseph I. Kemp* in, Captain Gage. Ship named after Fore River Ship Yard pilot, who had USS *Lexington* and other naval vessels on trial trips.

January 29th, USAT *Gen. George S. Simonds* (ex-USS *Great Northern*), Captain Mikklesen, ex-skipper of (Farrell) Bark *Tusitala*, with 1,700 negro laborers. Pilot of her in World War I.

February 21st, USS *Vesuvius*, AE-15, Captain George, in to Earle. Marian picked me up. Had swell dinner at Ye Cottage Inn, Keyport. $3.85 complete.

February 22nd, motor vessel *Henry Dundas* to sea. Loaded with high-octane gas and kerosene. Last ship in convoy. Dense fog.

February 27th, appointed with Pilot Bill Mitchell to study Safety Measures. Met with Hilton Lowe, Edgar Anderson, Bill Mitchell, Captain Lie of Marine Hearing Unit at Fraunces Tavern, had lunch. Jane and Marian typed my final report on Safety Plan. Off 10 days.

March 15th, T2 tanker *Hegra* out. Loaded with 100-octane gas. 55 ships, dense fog.

March 19th, had 70 ships in, 100 out.

March 23rd, steamship *Thomas Eakins* out, Captain Dodge. 31 feet draft (Liberty ship). Commodore.

April 13th, steamship *Patrick B. Whelan* out, Captain Ingenito. 77 ships. Delayed 4 hours by fog.

It was April 13, 1945 that the T2 steamship *St. Mihiel*

arrived at Ambrose Channel light vessel loaded with high-test gas. We put Pilot A. Buck (T) aboard and he proceeded in to port. The ship had a hole in her starboard side, leaking gas, and her midship section had been made useless by fire.

Captain Buck conned the ship from the bow from which point phone had been strung aft, to the engine and steering rooms. Fortunately, it was clear and conditions were good, so she finally anchored in the lower Statue Anchorage, still leaking gas out of the wound in her side. A patrol of Coast Guard picket boats was set up and no one was allowed near the vessel to reduce the danger of fire. She had left New York in a fast 16-knot convoy bound for Europe, and two days later, April 9, 1945, she was rammed by the tanker *Nashbulk*, whose steering gear failed. The midships house and bridge was ablaze at once, and relief Captain Porter and 26 crew men lost their lives. The ship was abandoned, but the next day Second Officer Bruno B. Baretich and other crew members boarded the disabled craft and put out the fire, saving the tanker and 5,000,000 gallons of gasoline. She returned to New York with bridge, midships section, telegraphs, steering gear, and radio completely destroyed. These men all received commendations and medals.

I arrived the following day aboard an inbound Liberty ship, *M.M. Guhin*, with 352 "Kraut" prisoners, part of a huge convoy, and with ships anchored all over picking an anchorage was a problem. I pointed out a nice clear berth ahead of a loaded tanker at the Statue to the skipper, but was later warned off by a Coast Guard picket boat. He cursed them up hill and down dale for not letting us anchor in what we thought was a clear berth, so we finally dropped the hook in close to quarters, further along. I was later waiting for a boat to take me ashore when the same picket boat hailed me, asking if the pilot wanted to go ashore. I said yes, went down the ladder, and once aboard was greeted of all things by Lt. Commander "Monks" Hart, former Curtis High schoolmate of 1907-08, whom I hadn't seen in years. I asked him why we were denied an anchorage near the tanker. He said no vessel was permitted within 600 feet, as the high-test gas was still leaking out of her side profusely, and highly dangerous. After talking over old times over a shot of Java, I was landed at Battery.

The *St. Mihiel* was later renamed *Camp Verde.*

April 16th, submarine USS 95, R-18 to sea—Captain Moree.

April 20th, to sea on pilot boat *Wanderer*, 58 men. U-boat sunk off Point ZED.

April 24th, lights go on in Britain after 5 years.

April 25th, to sea on pilot boat *Wanderer*, 57 men.

April 27th, steamship *William Ford Nichols* in, Captain Haymaker, Commodore Cohen. All coastal vessels still convoyed. Subs still busy.

May 2nd, motor vessel *Fernplant* to anchor, then to sea. Had breakfast with Ambassador to Turkey, Mr. & Mrs. Wilson, an Austrian Countess. Also Ambassador to Iran, Mr. Murray and his wife. Very interesting.

May 3rd, 8 munitions ships recalled from sea.

May 6th, U-boat sank collier *Black Point* off Point Judith. Admiral Doenetz orders subs to quit. I had USS APA-115, Hampton, Captain Ferguson, to sea, bound to Norfolk in convoy. Had American collier *Sewalls Point*, Captain Gross, in to anchor in collier anchorage. Was convoyed from Norfolk. Subs busy to the last.

May 8th, 12:01 A.M. European War ends. Lights on.

May 9th, I had minesweeper USS YMS-460 out from Pier 8, Staten Island, for maneuvers, sweeping practice off Old Orchard Shoal with two other minesweepers. Had Russian officers and an American interpreter. I was teacher and the Russians did the work. U.S. government turned 5 sweepers over to the Russians.

May 10th, German naval units and subs surrender to the British.

May 19th, 45 men stand by for sailings, 100 due.

May 20th, Marian and I watch USS *Benevolence* sail from Pavilion Hill, George Neumiller aboard. USS *Mt. Vernon* arrives, docks at Pier 16 Staten Island with happy returning boys (Washington).

May 22nd, all U.S. Army docks being repainted in bright colors. Large Welcome Home sign at Ft. Hamilton, Highland, and Sandy Hook Light.

May 28th, Pilot Jack Jenkins had German U-boat in to Pier A, Battery. Used for 7th War Bond Rally.

May 29th, convoys finished!! Hurray!! Staten Island cleared out—everybody happy. Nets and mines being removed.

June 3rd, steamship *John Henry* in with 6,000 tons of explosives. Leonardo to England and return. Captain Sullivan.

June 5th, convoy of 29 ships arrive in O.N. Convoy.

June 15th, old World War II system of flag hoists finished; new four-flag hoist is in. I got tobacco ration card.

June 17th, King George leaves on HA-13, *Benevolence*, from Norfolk.

June 19th, General Eisenhower received in great style by N.Y. City.

June 20th, Outside Guard Boat, Fire Island Light Vessel, West Gate Boat and Nets, Buoy 19 removed. Steamship *Queen Mary* arrives with 14,626 happy returning troops—Great Welcome.

July 14th, PEACE War ends 7:00 P.M. People go wild—me too!!!

July 17th, Swedish and other foreign ships in peacetime colors. Motor vessel *John Ericsson* (ex-*Kingsholm*) sails with full load of civilian passengers. First since the war.

July 25th, USS *Benevolence* with 400 other ships at Sangami Bay, Tokyo.

July 30th, our Navy has sunk over 1,000 assorted Japanese vessels in the last three weeks. Our fliers destroyed or damaged 2,600 aircraft.

August 7th, we drop first Atom Bomb—on Hiroshima.

August 8th, *New York Herald Tribune* prints Shipping News again.

August 10th, Pilot Paul Cullison's brother dies in Marine Hospital. Was torpedoed on Murmansk run. Frozen in lifeboat.

With uniformed pilot Carl Huus and an apprentice in the stern, a boat's crew makes this heavy yawl fly.

August 12th, motor tanker *Black Rock*, Captain Verleger, out. . . towing two barges loaded with beer. Bound to South Pacific.

It was a nice day, August 26, 1945, that I took a brand new DD-713, USS *Bailey*, to sea where we calibrated the D.F. adjusted compasses with degaussing on and off. We had finished the job with Mr. Tribble making out his cards down below and the pilot boat *New Jersey* out ahead, had sent a motorboat to take us off. The captain had sent for his sidearms, and when they were brought to him he put them on.

I was standing in the center of the bridge, watching the approaching motorboat with the skipper to my right, adjusting his belt. He took the .45 out of the holster, examined it, pointed it down, just clear of my feet, and pulled the trigger. There was a roar as the gun went off, and I was too surprised to be scared. The skipper, a swell guy, was at a loss for words and a bit embarrassed. A detail was sent below to see if anyone was injured; also to see what had happened to the bullet. The deck, being of steel, must have deflected it, and it couldn't have missed me by much.

By this time the motorboat was alongside, the skipper thanked me, and we shook hands as I wished him good luck with his new charge. I left feeling that luck had been with me.

September 1st, Japanese sign surrender aboard USS *Missouri*. VJ Day. Port Director control ends.

October 13th, steamship *William D. Pender*, Captain Burns, in with 915 troops. All troopships met by reception launch with band and pretty girls.

October 17th, part of the Pacific Fleet arrives, led by carrier USS *Monterey*, Pilot George Oldmixon. Also *Enterprise*, *Bataan*, cruiser *Portland*, and 6 destroyers. Came along 4:40 A.M. on a beautiful clear night. Beautiful sight.

October 28th, Dalzell tugs moved 62 vessels, mostly navy.

November 20th, steamship *Wm. Pepperell* to sea.

Captain Moodie of Eltingville, Staten Island, only 23 years old. All food rationing except sugar ends.

November 28th, steamship *Sea Scorpion*, Captain Bailey, to sea. Easterly gale. Pilot boat *New Jersey* and motorboats up on pilot boat *New York* on station. Waited 4 1/2 hrs to be taken off at Ambrose Channel light vessel. The *New York* very busy and a mess.

It was November 28, 1945, the wind east, gale force, and I was second five o'clock man, Cliff Lowe, who lived in Long Island, being first. I considered myself lucky to be home on a night like this, when suddenly the phone rang. It was the Office, and I was informed that the steamship *Sea Scorpion*, anchored off Stapleton, wanted a pilot immediately to take him to sea. Cliff Lowe, way out on Long Island couldn't make it, so it was my baby.

Marian drove me to Stapleton, where boatman Bobby Schmeiser put me aboard. In going off I thought, "this ship won't get underweigh in a gale like this," but I was wrong, for when I met Captain Baily, he said, "All ready, Pilot," and away we went, after heaving in 90 fathom of chain. We proceeded to sea, visibility good, wind east, gale force, tremendous sea, with pilot boat *New York* alone on station, no motorboats. She was busy boarding and taking out men. We lay hove to off Ambrose light vessel with a good lee on the starboard side, the ship being loaded.

The hours passed, but the skipper was very patient, for which I was glad, for the ship was bound to the Far East, a trip I didn't relish. Finally, after four and a half hours, the *New York* rounded to under her lee, dropped her yawl whose light was soon extinguished. We could see the yawl approaching in the glare of the *New York*'s searchlight, and I had my fingers crossed for the boys pulling the oars, they being inexperienced. They got alongside safely, but couldn't light the yawl light. Having Pilot Dewey McIntyre in mind (he and two boys lost their lives because they had no light), I asked the mate for his flashlight, which he gave me and I still have.

We got back to the *New York* safely, the boys doing very well, considering. The *New York* was a mess and was I glad to get aboard a loaded tanker for a passage with Pilot Paul Cullison at daybreak, bound back.

December 1st, disenrolled from U.S. Coast Guard (R)(T). In civvies.

It was December 6, 1945, and the T2 tanker *Santa Fe Hills* was anchored on Bay Ridge Flats, just below the Bay Ridge Channel. She and other tankers were to lay up due to lack of cargoes, when suddenly there was a change of orders. I was assigned to this vessel, and the captain and I were hustled aboard by Eddie Johnson of Stapleton Launch and prepared to sail for the Gulf at once. The skipper invited me into his spacious room and office and bade me to make myself comfortable while he unpacked. He said all this was unexpected, and he had his wife pack his suitcases in a hurry. These lay on his big bed and he started to unpack. I was seated in a chair, and after awhile he said, "Guess my wife must have put this gun in with my clothes," as he displayed an automatic .38. He stood before me, trying to remove the cartridge clip, telling me it wasn't loaded.

He was having a time with it, and the gun was pointed in my direction, quite often making me nervous, so I said, "Skipper, will you kindly point that gun away from me?" He did by going into the bathroom.

After awhile he came out with the clip removed and sheepishly remarked, "Look, Pilot, she was fully loaded all the time!"

This was lesson #3 for me and taught me to treat all "empty" guns as if they were loaded and never point a gun at anyone.

December 22nd, my son Ed (also a pilot) arrived from Havre on old USS *George Washington*.

On Friday December 28, 1945 the steamship *Pure Oil*, inward bound from Marcus Hook, arrived at a point about 2 miles south southeast from the Gedney buoy and desired a pilot. The weather was calm, sea smooth, visability about 3 miles. I put off in our motorboat and went alongside on the starboard side. The ship, flying light, draft 16 feet aft, about 10 feet amidships and 5 feet forward, had a ladder composed of two sections over about amidships. I mounted the ladder, climbed up several rungs, when the entire lower section broke free causing me to fall with it, striking the lower part of my spine on the rail of the motorboat, my left knee against the ship's side and my head down between the motorboat and the ship's side. I was temporarily stunned and pulled clear by our two boys. The ladder and my Stetson drifted astern, and after recovering my senses, I ordered another ladder put over, went aboard, took the ship to anchor off Staten Island. My trousers and coat had quite some of the ship's bottom paint on them which the Captain had removed. He regretted the accident and offered his help as did other members of the crew. The pain and soreness increased and upon arriving home I went to bed at once.

The lower section of the ladder was recovered by our boat and upon examination it was found that the lashing of the lower section had been hitched to the lower wooden rung of the upper section instead of to the side roping. The wooden checks holding this rung pulled out of the roping, causing the lower section to fall.

Pilots daily experience poor, broken, unrepaired ladders, poorly secured or cock-billed ladders, ladders that are hung by catching a rung over a cleat on the rail without a lashing, ladders with slack in them that drop when weight is put on them. In my 37 years in the N.Y. Pilot Service I have never feared climbing a ladder under any conditions, gales, heavy seas, ice, etc., but I do now, realizing that my life (and the lives of my shipmates) might be snuffed out or ruined through someone's carelessness or ignorance.

In this U. S. Coast Guard photo, Pilot Harold Kaiser, in his Coast Guard uniform, stands on the flying bridge of a Liberty ship during winter convoy duty in New York Harbor. (Courtesy Howard Hill)

Appendix
Pilots Reminisce with Edward Winters

From the late 1940s to the early 1960s, several retired pilots sent reminiscences of their service to Edward Winters. Pilot John Ronayne (1876-1957), sent an annual Christmas card and other messages, beginning in 1948. Each year he reminisced about his early experiences, giving a picture of piloting under sail in the 1890s and early 1900s.

Christmas 1948

AHOY Shipmate!

Well here we are, in for another Christmas, and it makes me think back to 1906, off Fire Island. I was one of the cruising men, and there were only three of us left on #3. I had the last turn. There were Mr. Berry, Jim's father, and Mr. Germond. It was blowing hard from the west, and quite some sea. We were under double-reefed foresail and head of the staysail, with the main boom in the crotch, thinking of setting the main trysail. The cook was trying his skill in cooking a turkey with no after sail on the boat, stove won't draw, so had to set trysail if we wanted turkey. Just finished dinner when the watch reported a brig on the port tack reaching to the north. It was awful cold and we had some ice on the deck and rigging. Mr. Germond had the turn, went on deck to have a look. Brig was under lower topsail, reefed foresail, and two-reef mainsail making heavy weather of it, and had a jack flying. I asked Mr. Germond if I could have the turn, and he said, "You sure can." So down in the cabin I go, carved a whole leg, wing, and some breast, wrapped them in newspaper, stuffed them into my bag along with some chestnuts, oranges, and apples. The captain would have given me the brig, had it belonged to him, for my gift. I wish you could have seen him. Well, to finish the story, we made our reach to Long Island, and wore ship just west of Shinnecock in about five fathoms. I was going to put upper topsail on her, but it coming on dark I was glad I didn't, for we hove to at midnight under a goose-wing lower topsail, and boy, did it blow. At daylight it moderated some, then we made more sail, with jibs, upper and lower topsails, and single-reef mainsail. We were well south of Barnegat, land not in sight, when we wore ship to port tack. Wind hauled toward evening of second night to west southwest. We reached Quarantine at noon. Two days of hard work for a 14-foot pilotage—some work for flat tires.

Christmas 1949

(picture of ship *A.J. Fuller*)

Dear Ed,

This ship—*A.J. Fuller*—we put Mr. W. Ferrie aboard of her a little east of Nantucket in a strong breeze of east northeast wind. We had been running to the westward under easy sail with one pilot aboard, when we made the ship reaching to the northward on the starboard tack. We made sail, gave chase and spoke her. She said, "Yes, but no offshore pilotage" (an additional 25 percent charge). Mr. Ferrie told the captain to back his main yard and he would come aboard. It would have done your heart good to hear the orders for heaving to— "Haul main sail up—down jib topsail—clew up main royal— stand by weather main braces—hard down the wheel—shiver the main yards." Mr. Ferrie aboard, hauled in the main braces and filled away—jib topsail—mainsail—sailor aloft to overhaul clewlines and buntlines, reset skysail and royal. We put everything we had on the *Loubat*, but at sunset all we could see of the *Fuller* was her skysail and royals. She was loaded with chalk from England for ballast. The year was April 1894. They were some times. The *Fuller* must have been making 15 knots as we were doing 10 or 11 knots. The weather was a dry easterly and very clear.

Christmas 1950

Dear Ed,

We will soon be on another long tack for New Year and I hope it will be good one, as this tack we are on has not brought us to windward, and let us hope the wind will change and be fair. I was out to see Harry Miller and he was sure happy to see me. . . . Harry and I were boys in the *Lawrence* #4, that was after the consolidation. He certainly was a nice shipmate. He wanted to be remembered. Those were the happy days, and I remember one stormy night with the wind east, the old Italian bark *Maria de Albuno* burned a torch and backed her main yard. Mr. Ferrie went aboard for our last man. He was no sooner aboard, when he came to the rail and called Harry and I alongside and told us to tell the boatkeeper to follow him in and keep close as the bark was taking water very fast and might capsize. We stood by, and when we got to Staten Island, Mr. Ferrie anchored on the Tail of the Flats in three fathoms of water. Mr. Ferrie told us afterwards that when he got in smooth water the bark didn't leak so bad that they couldn't get the best of it. What made it so bad for the crew of the bark was that they had no lifeboats, as they were all smashed in a previous gale they had, which strained the bark so that some of her planks on the side were opened up. Well they were lucky that night that we were there and got a pilot like Mr. Ferrie.

Christmas 1951

Hello Ed,

Almost another year has passed and I begin to look back at the years I spent in pilot boats and the things that took place. I was in the *Joseph F. Loubat* #16; she was named after one of the big men of the French Line. In July 1893 we were well down east off soundings, that meant 62 degrees or 63 degrees, in dense fog which we had fought for two days. Heard a steamer blowing, but never saw him and finally the fog lifted and close to us was the New Jersey pilot boat *Thomas S. Negus* #1. Also in sight was the Anchor Line steamship *Furnessia* loaded with passengers. We both shook out reefs and under full sail gave chase. We had a bit of advantage on the *Negus*, but on the next tack one of her sailors, in hauling on the main sheet, fell overboard. She kept right on, but Mr. Ferrie, who was at the wheel of our boat, went to the rescue. We "out yawl" and got him just in time. Saving him cost us the ship. His name was Lars Nelson, and I shall never forget that instant. They sure were tough men. . . . I heard the pilots of the *Loubat* talking about it, and I think when it came before the Board they had to pass the pilotage over to the *Loubat*. I wonder if the young pilots of today know what the older pilots went through.

April 15, 1952

Dear Ed,

Just received your letter and I am glad you found out it was three headsails on #7, because all pilot boats (built) had forestaysail, jib, and jib topsail, except one, the *Actea* #15. She was a yacht, and I was in her a short time. That was the pilot boat that Gene McCarthy was spare boy in, before the pilots consolidated in 1895. When she was sold, he went into the *Adams*. She was a steam bunker man, and the first steamboat in the business. Joe Bigley was boat keeper. The pilots live forward and the crew aft. She sure was some vessel, had a draft of eight feet, could do some rolling, and was full of rats. Joe used to pick off a rat that was crawling along the rudder chains and throw it in the bunk opposite, and it was a tossup who was out of the bunk first—the man or the rat. Gosh, the funny things that used to happen. . . . I will tell you some other time what happened when Captain Dennis Reardon, Jersey Pilot, and Oscar Stoffreiden read the writing on the deck outside the main companionway, sure was hell. I left and shipped in a brig called the *Harriet G*. She was owned by Captain Miller. You knew him; he was in the Ward Line for years. . . . He sure did make a sailor out of me and we had many long talks when we laid overnight in Quarantine. You wrote about your father's boat . . . . She was lost in a gale, went ashore in Newport, Rhode Island, on the rocks and broke up. That was after your father's time was out and he was a pilot. I heard pilots say if your father had been there it would not have happened. Mr. Winters was a sailorman, and I always admired him and paid attention to everything he told. I remember when I was boat keeper of the *Washington* #5. I anchored close inshore, off Stapleton. We had no wind, drifted up, and when I let go we were well inshore of the Long Dock. During the night a three-masted schooner anchored off our starboard quarter. Being the first of the month I had to go to the office to sign bills and get wages while the boys were busy with a month's store of coal and wood. In the meantime, while I was in New York at the office, the wind hauled to northeast and was blowing quite fresh, when we were ordered off. Mr. Sayles had the turn and your father was one of the Company of Pilots. Oh boy—there was the boat laying in ebb tide, the schooner still there on our starboard quarter. It seemed impossible to get out of this hole until the flood tide made.

Mr Sayles gave me hell for anchoring the boat there, but

he didn't know how it happened, and I took it all until your father in his nice quiet way said to Mr. Sayles—Why not let the boat keeper get her underway?"

Your father held back and asked me if I needed his help, and I told him I would "Box Haul" her on the headsails. I had all my boys trained that when an order was given and I repeated it, it was carried out. Well, we hove the anchor short, had forestaysail and jib ready to hoist, sheets made fast to windward, as we could not have any headway on account of the schooners. I went aft, put the wheel up, got the wind on the port bow, up jib, up staysail, hove anchor off the bottom, and cleared the schooner by ten feet. I'm going by the schooner, the captain must have been watching the maneuver, for he called out to me just as Mr. Sayles reached the deck from below. He heard him say "Nice piece of seamanship," and the other pilot heard it too, and do you know, Mr. Sayles never spoke to me from that day to the day he died. Your father said I didn't miss much, and I think he was right. When we cleared the schooner we went to sea with a single-reef foresail and double-reefed mainsail, and I was relieved when we reached the lightship and hove to. They were the good old days. I guess all the boys I had with me with the exception of a few, have crossed the River Jordan: Harry Arnold, Johnny Swainson, Johnny Kiernan, Hughie McIntyre, Billy Canvin (he went with Charlie Peterson in #3), Carl Huus, Frank Miller, Freddy Fendt, Joe M. Sullivan, and Arthur Peterson came with me on my last three or four months that I had to serve. All of them came as spare boys, and everyone of them became a first-class pilot. There was no nonsense and everyone knew his place. Going back to Mr. Sayles—we were coming in "manned" from the eastward late one February afternoon, the wind east northeast, quite a breeze, under single-reef sails with fine, light snow. At the Whistling Buoy the *New York* spotted us and dropped her flag, so I hove to and my friend, Mr. Sayles, came aboard—alone—without a word. Filled away on course for Gedney Channel (Back of Romer was closed to navigation), getting dark, with Tom Port and Johnny Swainson on lookout for buoys; Carl Huus casting the lead. Made Buoys of the Middle, almost alongside of it before we saw it, as snow killed the sound of the bell, just missed it. When it did ring, my friend, Mr. Sayles, came bounding up the companionway and wanted to know what buoy that was and ordered me to take the boat to an anchor "Back of the Bank."

We were hauled up on course with lee rail underwater, and I told him we were bound for Staten Island, that the boat was manned, and that was where we were bound. He stormed a bit, and I would have given a cookie to know what he thought. Up off Staten Island (Stapleton) there was a bark and a full-rigged ship at anchor, and I knew they were still there as there had been no offshore wind for them to sail. Still snowing, I made Ft. Tompkins Light, could see the glimmer of Quarantine lights, and with my two lookout men still on the job, tide flood, wind east strong, and snow, made the bark, then the ship. Tacked under the stern, when Mr. Sayles came on deck, took one look, and started shouting to let go of the anchor. Because of no repeat from me, no anchor. I powered mainsail, took in forestaysail, jib, and then foresail, came to anchor off Stapleton in our old berth. Hove out the yawl and put our friend ashore. Put the forty-five in the water, furled the sails, hoisted the yawl in on the deck to keep snow out of it, put up curtain (weather cloth) this was a piece of canvas that stretched across the main hatch, to keep out draught and snow. We made wonderful time up. It was 4:30 P.M. when we left the pilot boat *2*, anchored at 6:30 P.M., and next morning there was a foot and a half of snow on the deck. Mr. Paul Woudrige, President, told me he would hold me personally responsible for the boat when she was manned. I went to the Office next day, had the log with me, which had to be notarized before presenting to the secretary, Mr. Nash. A complaint had been lodged, but was dismissed by Mr. Woudrige, who said I was only carrying out orders.

Christmas 1952

Dear Ed,

It was the year 1902. I was boat keeper of the *Washington #5* and was in hopes we would get up for Christmas ashore, but could not make it. We had a heavy northwest gale for five days and all the ships were held back, then the wind hauled to north and very cold. We had Messrs. Pratt, Yates, and Berry on board, and they decided to anchor under Long Island Beach to keep from icing up. We got to anchor just before supper and all felt pretty down. No one was talking, and I was writing in the log. The cook was fixing up the turkey for the next day. After supper about 7:00 P.M. the cabin door opened and Mr. Berry invited all hands aft. He had a couple of bottles of good rye, and we were all singing, even Mr. Yates, and that was the first and last time I ever saw him drink; well Christmas Eve wasn't so bad. We got underway after coffee in the morning. The wind was northeast strong, with three steamers in sight. We had the turkey for ourselves and Christmas night ashore.

February 8, 1953

Hi Ed,

Well, Ed, I see by the papers the boys are having their own trouble with the towboat strike. I know you and I had a few before we gave up, but there were some good jobs and some bad. I remember one, the *City of Dakar*, from Pier 4, Bush Docks, to DeVoe's, Long Island City, to load caseoil. She was the third ship in. Well, when I saw where she laid, with two ships astern, two ships on Pier 5, and all sorts of lighters, I didn't think I could get her out. When I got aboard, and the captain said he didn't think we could move, I told him I would try. The mates were fine fellows, all young and what a help they were; nothing was trouble for them. They got the crew to move some lighters astern for us; put them under our bow. Spring over, bow off, clear of ship that lay astern, and got a line to her to straighten us out. There was a channel not very wide, and we, being in ballast, with a big side out of water, had to be careful of our stern. Boy was I glad when we reached the end of Pier 4, bound up to DeVoe's. You know it is a slack-water job, as the ships have to be head-down on the bulkhead. Well, all the time it took at the Bush Docks, we were 1 1/2 hours late, and the tide was strong flood. I told the chief officer that we would let go of the anchor, and as the ship swung to it, try not to part the chain, also have the port anchor ready. Before I got to Newtown Creek, I had the ship stopped and we were going up quite fast on the tide. I kept to the westward as far as possible, and reaching the Sugar House, put the wheel hard right, full ahead, then full astern and "let go." Half ahead, her head swinging and the anchor dragging, Blackwell's Island was going by over the stern by knots. After 60 fathoms of chain was out the ship brought up abreast of the bulkhead, head to the tide, hove up anchor and made landing. I know we could not have left Bush Docks if it weren't for the help of the mates and crew. Just think, that was a $10 job with all the thrill thrown in. I know you had the same. The time for transporting was 9:00 A.M., and we finish at 1:00 P.M., but I was aboard at 8:00 A.M. as you know the rule was one hour before sailing time. I wonder if it is the same now.

Christmas 1955

Hi Shipmates !

Will shake out some reefs and put on all sail and tell you some about our trip to South America. We had a fine trip, fine weather, even crossed the equator in a dead calm. Our first call was Bahia—10 degrees south. I was in that port 62 years ago in the brig *Harriet G.*, Captain Miller of the Ward Line, who taught me how to be a sailor. And I didn't meet him again until I was a pilot in 1908, when I happened to get aboard the steamship *Monterey*, his first command in steam. We were both surprised to meet again, and he told me he sold the brig to the Alaska Salmon Co. and took her around Cape Horn to Seattle, making a smart passage.

I was paid off from the *Harriet G.* and went into the pilot boat *Joseph F. Loubat* #16. In 1895 we were off Georges Shoals, that is east of Nantucket, reefing down preparing for a northwest gale, when the pilot boat *George H. Warren* passed us under full sail. That night at 12 o'clock we were under fore and main trysails, blowing a gale. The *Warren* was never seen again, all hands lost.

Christmas 1956

Hi Ed,

I remember back in 1910, I went aboard the White Star Liner *Arabic* at 7:00 P.M. The weather wasn't so nice with plenty of wind from the north and cold. She was anchored in Quarantine with four shackles [60 fathoms of chain] in the water. I told the captain to have the second anchor ready and to keep a good watch on the ship, that she did not drag. He then told me they had only one anchor, as when they were getting the anchors ready at sea something went wrong with the port anchor, and it let go and they lost it with 30 fathom of chain. He was thinking of staying outside and enter port at daylight, but weather was looking bad. He decided to take on a pilot and anchor in Harbor. I was given a nice room and was thankful to be lucky in getting a nice ship. I wasn't in bed long before an officer was at my bedside, telling me the ship was dragging and to hurry to the bridge, which I did. The captain was there, and engines were going ahead. Well we were down past the Narrows before we got the anchor and got a nice clear berth off Stapleton in 7 fathoms. We kept the engines on ahead slow to take some of the strain off the anchor chain. To make it worse, it began to snow, and I never passed a longer night waiting for daylight. Wasn't I glad to see the doctor's boat heave up anchor and head for 61 North River. I think if the ship had dragged again, the captain would have ordered me to take her back to sea. I think I drank about 20 cups of tea during my turn on the bridge, and she had one of those wheelhouses that was open at both ends and no doors, sure was a cold place. I was lucky to have her out to sea the day before Christmas, and when I looked in my bag it sure was heavy. I had plenty of Christmas cheer and a letter from Captain Davis wishing me a "Merry Christmas."

As Ever
John

Pilot John Hauffman wrote in January 1960, recalling some of his most memorable experiences.

Hi Shipmate,

You have asked for a few instances that stand out in the game of piloting, here they are.

No. 1: The sailing of the five-masted schooner from sea to Quarantine anchorage, getting underweigh and sailing her up to 34th Street, North River, to an anchorage. Three months later when orders came in to sail to sea from an anchorage off of 34th Street I got her again. It was December 18th, 5:00 P.M. when I got aboard, blowing hard from the northwest. The skipper informed me he would like to sail, and as the wind was 30 mph he was sure she would handle alright. I said, "Let's go," so we could save as much daylight as possible, of which there was nil. She was drawing 24 feet, and I sailed her down the bay, and figured on the heel, glided through Swash Channel to Sea, no trouble. When I got aboard the pilot boat, they told me I was crazy.

No. 2: The British steamship *Empress of Scotland* (ex-*Kaiserin Auguste Victoria*—4 masts, 2 funnels). I boarded the ship laying at Cunard Line Pier, ebb tide, thick fog, draft of 32 feet. Captain Wolfe, Superintendent, told me the ship had to make time, and anything I could do to expedite her trip would be appreciated. I told him it was a tough job, but if he would not dump all the ash cans in New York on me, I would take the ship to sea. Well, I did. Boy, the first thing I did I nearly landed in St. George Ferry slip, got her out, just cleared a man-o-war bow. Believe me, I was having kittens, but I could not anchor as there were more bells ringing than there were churches in Brooklyn, so out I went. Heard two strong bells ahead; told Captain Ahearn there were two ships there, or one with a bell fore and one aft, and as it was too late to anchor if we hit amidships it would be an easy hit as we were going full astern. Well it turned out to be two ships and, mind you, I could not see the bow of the *Empress*, and the first thing I knew I took the bow off of the steamship *Scottsburg* with my starboard quarter and damaged our lifeboats.

After I cleared the fog lifted, entered the channel, had fog of same density and on the second leg heard a bell and, knowing it to be ebb tide, figured she would be up and down channel, not thinking she would be on my side, and lo and behold it was a tanker. They dropped fenders over the side and we slipped by. Brother, we gasped for breath, and after we cleared

Captain Ahearn said another one like that and they would pick him up from the bridge. I told him he would not be the only one on his back; I would be there too. Well, after I got aboard the boat, I was wringing wet, and that night the White Star Liner *Olympic* came along and I swapped for her. Went aboard, still thick as tar, and Captain Binks told me he had 1,200 bags of mail aboard which was supposed to be landed that night. I told him what had happened to the *Empress*. He said he knew and asked if I had lost my nerve. I said no, but he would yell quits before me. Well, we proceed up, flood tide, we got as far as Craven Shoal, and with all the whistles and bells, you would think it was New Years. He said, "Anchor you damn fool, or we will all be shaking hands in jail for manslaughter." We did; it was 1:00 A.M.

No. 3: Had a Danish freighter bound to Albany; got as far as Catskill Bridge when it shut in. It was about 6:00 P.M., flood tide, and with some dredging going on ahead I had to judge my distance there as I saw a red flag displayed before it shut in. I knew it meant dynamite, and I was not ready to meet my maker. Well, six hours later (midnight) we were fast to the pier in Albany, still thick.

No. 4: I had a tedious job towing a dead ship loaded with scrap, drawing 27 feet. It took three days and two nights before I anchored off Staten Island, 8:00 P.M. The captain of the tug told me several towboat companies refused the job, so he had to come all the way from Helgoland here to do the job, and I was the dumbbell. Towed all the way from Albany without incident.

As for World War II, heard they wanted a docking pilot out in the Far East (Okinawa), so I applied for the job. Was turned down due to pump. They wanted me to go to New Orleans and take charge of ships in yard; I refused as I wanted to see action. They contacted the army base and had me join up there. After drilling over there for a few months, I took

250 men overseas to man towboats and get them ready for D Day. Well, I split them in ten ports and got the boats ready, which I thought was all I was to do, but no, I had to take groups of eighteen boats through the Irish Sea to Southampton then crisscross England to London for orders. While I was in headquarters in London a buzz bomb came over; this was my first experience and as the alarm sounded they all ran for cover. I stayed in my chair, and when it was over the colonel said to me, "Gee, you have nerve." Nerve, hell, I did not know where to go, and my legs would not move. Maybe that is what I got one of the citations for from President Truman after the war. The other one must have been for bringing a convoy safely from Hull to Southampton through the North Sea in a hell of a gale, with fighting overhead and I prayed to fight up there and not come too close to us as all we had was potatoes to fling at subs and aircraft.

Two weeks after returning to the States, I was made superintendent of Pier 1, Army Base, then shifted to Pier 84, North River, where it was a madhouse. They wanted me to go to the Canal Zone and take charge of piers there. I quit; I had enough.

Pilot Leon Oldmixon wrote of his early years in the sailing pilot boats.

We have lost two more of our friends, Christian Wood and Harry Miller. Harry had just been made a pilot when I first came in the business in 1900. He had a long life and was an outstanding member and honor to the Association. I often wonder as I get older, who will be next? Speaking of the first time I came into the business, I recall that in 1900 during July and August I was given a vacation and took the occasion of returning to Buffalo, New York, my hometown. While I was there for two weeks, President McKinley was assassinated and my boat No. 7 was cut in two off the Highlands on a beautiful afternoon, and three or four pilots were drowned, as well as the cook. . . . In the winter of 1900-1901 I had a rather close call. We had orders to lay No. 7 up at Brady's Dock, Staten Island, on account of the great amount of ice in the bay. My brother George was boat keeper. While getting the lines and mooring equipment I managed to go overboard. I had boots, heavy clothing, and oilskins on, and the amount of clothing on me saved my life for it took some time for the water to soak through, thus keeping me afloat. George and Hubrook jumped in the yawl and picked me up as I was scrambling onto a floating piece of ice. So after escaping that experience and the sinking of the boat, I decided to leave and go deep water. I was away eight years when the pilots asked me to return. I was then chief mate on the *Virginian*, of the Hawaiian Lines. When I left previously, George Seeth, John Swainson, Tom Port, and others were doing time. I became a deputy pilot ahead of them.

Pilot William A. Mitchell wrote in December 1961 of an incident in 1917, which he termed "piloting in a night of horrors with the anchor down."

It was December 1917 and a troop convoy was to depart—each vessel having a pilot aboard. The vessels had been anchored awaiting one vessel, the flagship, *Covington* (ex-German steamship *Cincinnati*). She was delayed (awaiting troops arriving from the West via train and hindered by a snowstorm reaching Hoboken). Finally after two days the *Covington* sailed from Hoboken and proceeded to an anchorage off Norton's Point. From here to the Statue all anchorages were jammed with vessels.

Regulations called for convoys to leave in darkness to avoid sightseeing from the shoreline. To my way of thinking this was wrong. This particular situation was made hazardous by holding such large ships as the *President Grant, Pocahontas, Covington*, and others to an anchor in a small area with a northeast gale with snow blowing, then shifting to the northwest gale about midnight. The *Covington* sent word at 7:00 P.M. for all vessels to prepare to proceed.

USS *President Grant* reported a coastwise coal tow across her bow, the tug and one barge on the starboard side with two barges on the port side. Cannot proceed; all vessels ordered to remain at anchor.

A warning was broadcast to keep a sharp lookout for a barge loaded with dynamite, no lights, adrift in Gravesend Bay. When the wind shifted to northwest most vessels dragged. The *Covington* had six fathoms over the stern, drawing 33 feet, anchored off of Norton's Point.

The only pilot boat on station left it and passed in at 9:00 P.M. for a harbor. If the convoy had not been delayed, about eight pilots would have spent Christmas aboard, if not sunk.

At 4:00 A.M. I, pilot of the *Covington*, suggested we give anchor alert to prepare to sea. The reports of various ships were horrifying.

The *Pocahontas* had a hole in the starboard bow awaiting cement to patch it up. The tanker with Alonzo Beebe aboard drifted into Pilot Frank Cramer's vessel. Charlie Devereaux on the *President Grant* still had the coal tow on his bow. Clyde boat dragged alongside USS *Illinois* in Gravesend. Dynamite barge still adrift. Oil tanker off Staten Island fouled Swedish bark and the two drifted through the net into Gravesend. The escort cruiser with no pilot got ashore on Craven Shoal. So the proceeding was halted and postponed until darkness after 7:00 P.M.

I had given the watch officer orders (on the quiet) to call me if he saw the pilot boat going to sea. This he did at 3:30 A.M., so I was all ready to go at 4:00 A.M. (still dark).

Under these conditions, with so many large vessels crammed into a small anchorage space, all hands on all the vessels were on standby, and with no pilot boat on station we pilots had something to worry about.

Finally at 7:00 P.M. (darkness) with all vessels cleared and repaired, rid of entanglements, the troop convoy proceeded to sea with a moderate northwest wind. All pilots disembarked—a tired lot.

Glossary

A.C. or Ambrose Channel—Navigation channel in Lower New York Bay, formerly the East Channel, which was dredged in 1908-14 and renamed for John W. Ambrose, a New York City businessman who raised the funds needed to dredge it. While the Main Ship Channel makes a dogleg around the shoals, the Ambrose Channel is deeper and runs straight between East Bank and Roamer Shoal, reducing the piloted distance by several miles.

Ambrose Channel Light Vessel or A.C.L.V—A lightship operated by the United States Light House Service at the entrance to New York Bay. Originally called the Sandy Hook light vessel, it served on a station established at the entrance to the navigation channel in 1823. When the more direct Ambrose Channel was opened in 1908, the station was renamed Ambrose.

Bayside Cut—The short, three-quarter-mile northwest-southeast leg of the Main Ship Channel inside of Sandy Hook and adjacent to Sandy Hook Bay.

Bight—A slightly receding bay or recess in a seacoast between comparatively distant headlands, or a long or gradual bend of a coastline, such as the New York Bight, the bend in the coastline between New Jersey and Long Island.

Bitt—A strong post of wood or iron for belaying, fastening, and working ropes, cables, and mooring lines.

Blue Riband—The virtual award for the ship holding the transatlantic speed record. For much of Edward Winters's career it was the *Mauretania*, superseded by the *Rex, Normandie,* and *Queen Mary.*

Bush Docks—The extensive shipping terminal built around 1910 in Brooklyn, north of Bay Ridge, with easy access to the Narrows by way of the Bay Ridge Channel.

Case Oil—Kerosene, which was shipped in tin cans, with two cans in each wooden case.

Caven Point—A point of land in the Upper Bay, in Bayonne, New Jersey, due west of the Statue of Liberty.

Chock—A heavy wooden or metal fitting secured on a vessel or on a wharf, having jaws through which line or cable passes, and for which it serves as a fairlead.

Club—The Pilot Club, which was active in the late 1800s when the office was in Manhattan. Not a typical social club, it was more like the concept of a European guild of pilots.

Clyde Line—A U.S. shipping company providing regular service between New York and Atlantic coast and Gulf ports from Pier 36, North River.

Glossary

Commodore Ship—In a convoy, the ship carrying the senior officer, whose decisions and orders controlled the convoy.

Convoy—During wartime, troops and war materiel were carried from the U.S. to Europe in convoys of ships with naval and Coast Guard protection to shield them from submarine attack. A convoy might include more than 100 ships. Each ship in a departing or entering convoy required a pilot, so the number of Sandy Hook Pilots, and the pace and hazard of their work, increased greatly in 1917-19 and 1941-45.

Craven Shoals—A small shoal in Lower New York Bay, just below the Narrows and east of Hoffman Island.

Degaussing—A process developed in Great Britain during World War II to demagnetize iron and steel ships to make them impervious to magnetic undersea mines. Wire coils were suspended around the ship's hull and a charge run through the wires, which was adjusted until it neutralized the magnetic attraction of the ferrous metal. The process was adopted by the U.S. in 1942, and a degaussing range was set up near Swinburne Island in the Lower Bay. Here, the charge was adjusted and the compass corrected as the ship ran over a measured range.

Donkey Engine—A small utility engine on a vessel's deck. It often has a revolving drum, around which a line would be wrapped for hauling. Unguarded, and with rudimentary brakes, donkey engines were the cause of many shipboard injuries and deaths.

Donkey's Breakfast—A shipboard mattress, which was typically stuffed with straw or Spanish Moss.

East Bank—A shoal in Lower New York Bay, south of Coney Island and on the east side of Ambrose Channel.

Erie Basin—A contained basin in Brooklyn between Red Hook and Gowanus Bay, that served as a wheat shipping facility during the 1800s, later becoming the site of shipbuilding and ship repair, Todd's Erie Basin.

Explosives Anchorage—During wartime, ships laden with ammunition were anchored in Gravesend Bay, south and east of the Narrows, to limit damage if they were to explode.

Flats—In general terms, shallow portions of an estuary. Sandy Hook Pilots used the term specifically in reference to an anchorage off Bay Ridge, Brooklyn, in the Upper Bay, also Bay Ridge Flats.

Flit—A popular early aerosol insecticide, which was sprayed with a long-handled "gun."

Fort Lafayette—A military installation first built in 1812 upon Hendrick's Bluff, a reef 200 yards from the Brooklyn shore in the Narrows. Originally called Ft. Diamond, it was replaced in 1825 by a new fort named after Alexander Hamilton, which was renamed Ft. Lafayette after the Marquis de Lafayette. It became known colloquially during World War I as Dynamite Island, where ships were required to offload explosives. Ft. Lafayette was removed in 1959-60 to prepare for the Brooklyn pier of the Verrazano Narrows Bridge.

Fort Wadsworth—The military complex on the Staten Island side of the Narrows, including the prominent granite fortification built 1847-65 and named Ft. Wadsworth from 1865 to 1902. It was then renamed Battery Weed and the entire complex was called Ft. Wadsworth.

Fulton Fish Market—Area on the Lower East Side of Manhattan, just below the Brooklyn Bridge, used for wholesale distribution of freshly caught fish.

Gantling or Gantline—Colloquial form of the term girtline, a rope rove through a single block at the lower masthead and used for hoisting and to set up the rigging.

Gate Boat—During wartime protection of New York Bay with an antisubmarine net suspended across the mouth, the gate boat was a U.S. Navy vessel that opened the gate in the net to allow ships through. Only ships that communicated the correct code by Morse flash were permitted through.

Gedney Channel—Navigation channel in Lower New York Bay named after the surveyor, U.S. Navy Lieutenant John S. Gedney, who charted it in 1835 for the first U.S. coastal survey.

Gob—Slang term for an ordinary U.S. Navy sailor.

Gravesend Bay—Area of Lower New York Bay fronting southern Brooklyn, where Gravesend was an early English settlement whose name alludes to the settlement at the mouth of the Thames River in England. Partially sheltered from the open sea by Norton Point, Coney Island, Gravesend Bay was used as an anchorage, particularly for ammunition ships during wartime.

Gunwales or gunnels—The uppermost strake, or run of planking, on a ship's side, or the reinforced upper edge of a boat's side.

Hedge Hog—A forward-firing antisubmarine depth charge weapon developed during World War II.

Hell Gate—A sharp turn and narrowing of the East River that connects Long Island Sound to the upper bay of New York Harbor. With its rocky ledges and fast-flowing tides, Hell Gate was a very dangerous hazard to all ships. Originally named by the Dutch *Horll* (swirl or whirlpool) *Gatt* (opening or passage).

Hell Gate Men—Pilots qualified to navigate vessels through Hell Gate.

Hoffman and Swinburne Islands—Two small islands several miles below the Narrows and a mile off Staten Island. These are the only manmade islands in New York Harbor. During the height of immigration by sea, they were used as a Quarantine Station and burial ground for diseased passengers. During World War II, Hoffman Island was used as a base to train Merchant Marine radio operators and Swinburne Island as the control center for degaussing (see this term).

Husing, Ted—According to the American Sportscasters Association Hall of Fame, Ted Husing was an early radio personality largely responsible for play-by-play broadcasting of baseball games.

Inside Boat—The Pilot term for the vessel used to ferry Pilots between the pier and the Station Boat offshore. Also, there is a seasonal change with the station boat used in the summer and the one used in the winter. There is always one large vessel at the pier undergoing maintenance.

Kedge—A light anchor used for moving a vessel from place to place. It is carried out to a distance from the vessel, dropped and hauled in, thereby causing the vessel to move towards the anchor. It is generally the smallest anchor on board.

L.V.—An abbreviation for Light Vessel or ship. In this writing, usually the Scotland or Ambrose light vessels, which were stationed off the entrance to New York Bay.

Glossary

Lazarette or Lazareth—A storage locker on board ship, generally aft of the after cabin in smaller vessels. The term comes from the Italian *Lazaretto*, a house, or sometimes a ship, used to quarantine sick people or malefactors.

Leonardo Pier—The large pier and munitions depot completed at Earle, Leonardo, New Jersey, on Sandy Hook Bay, in April 1942. It was also referred to as Weapons Station Earle.

Lyle Gun—A small cannon developed by the U.S. Life-Saving Service to fire a projectile attached to a hemp line from the beach over the spars of a stranded ship. The shot line was used to drag a heavier line to the ship, by which a trolley-like breeches buoy was used to haul the ship's people ashore. These guns could also be used on shipboard for throwing a line to another ship.

Mae West—A once popular slang term used during and after World War II for a personal flotation device (lifejacket). The profile of the bulky kapok-filled jacket was likened to the prominent bustline of the popular vaudeville and film actress Mae West.

Marian—Edward Winters's wife.

Narrows—The dividing point between the Upper and Lower Bays, where Staten Island and Brooklyn are only about a mile apart.

Net, see Submarine Net.

Newtown Creek—A tidal arm of the East River, extending four miles inland and forming part of the boundary between Brooklyn and Queens. Though only 200 feet wide, it is navigable and ships lined its industrial bulkheads.

North River—The local name for the Hudson River, and especially for the southern end of the river where it meets New York Bay, adjacent to Manhattan.

Northwest 3/4 West—The cardinal points, when steering by compass, for the first inbound leg of Ambrose Channel.

Occ—Abbreviation for occulting, as in a light signal with a timed flash. Most lighthouses and some lighted buoys have an occulting signal to distinguish them from others.

Old Dominion Line—A shipping company providing regular service between New York and Southern ports from Pier 25, North River.

Old Orchard Shoal—A shoal off the south shore of Staten Island in Raritan Bay.

"Oslo Heights"—In the 1930s and 1940s, a local nickname for Bay Ridge, Brooklyn, alluding to the large Norwegian population.

Outside Boat—The pilot vessel on station at the seaward entrance to the port near the Sandy Hook or Ambrose lightship, approximately seven miles east of Sandy Hook, seven miles south of Rockaway Beach, and twenty miles from the tip of Manhattan.

Outside Guard Boat—The vessel stationed on the outside of the submarine net, protecting the "gate."

Owl's Head—Colloquial name for the lighted buoy north of the Narrows, on the east side of the channel, opposite to the entrance to the Kill Van Kull.

Painter—A rope attached to the stem (bow) or stern of a boat and used for mooring to a pier or jetty or used to secure to another vessel.

Para Boat—A colloquial term for ships providing service between New York and Belem on the Para River branch of the Amazon in the state of Para on the north coast of Brazil.

Pavilion Hill—A prominent hill in northern Staten Island, also known as Grymes Hill.

Peruna—A popular patent medicine manufactured in Columbus, Ohio, and sold across the nation. A bottle contained about a half pint of 190-proof spirits, a pint and a half of water, some flavoring, and a little burnt sugar for coloring. A bottle of Peruna cost about 18 cents to manufacture and sold for $1.00.

Pilot—In general terms, one who navigates a vessel. Before World War II, the navigation officer on a British ship was called the pilot. More specifically, a pilot is one licensed to navigate ships within prescribed boundaries alongshore. Depending on the level of their rating, Sandy Hook Pilots are licensed to navigate vessels of specified drafts through some or all of the channels of the Port of New York and New Jersey.

Poorhouse Flats—Shoal water in the East River on the Manhattan shore just above the 23rd Street Landing.

Port Johnson—An important depot for anthracite coal carried from the mines of northeastern Pennsylvania to the shore by railroad. Located on the busy Kill Van Kull, almost across from Sailors' Snug Harbor on the north shore of Staten Island, it was a frequent subject for the marine artist John Noble.

Pratique (also see Radio Pratique)—Permission or license to proceed to discharge passengers granted by the port medical authorities to a vessel upon arrival from a foreign port after quarantine inspection. All ships from foreign ports that enter the Port of New York must be inspected for sick passengers and crew. Malaria, typhoid, small pox, and yellow fever were a continual threat in the 1800s.

Prince Line—A British steamship line managed by Furness, which provided service between New York and Africa, Asia, South America, and the Gulf ports.

Prohibition—The period from January 1920 to December 1933 when the U.S. outlawed alcoholic consumption through the National Prohibition Enforcement Act (Volstead Act) that provided enforcement provisions for the 18th Amendment to the Constitution. It was repealed by the 21st Amendment to the Constitution.

Q Ship—British vessel used as a decoy for German U-boats during World War I. Converted merchant and fishing vessels, with light armament, Q ships worked alone or with British submarines to attract and destroy U-boats. During the war, seven Q ships were sunk by U-boats, and fifteen U-boats were sunk by Q ships or British submarines.

Quarantine or Quarantine Station—A temporary anchorage on the Staten Island shore above the Narrows where incoming ships received a medical inspection. Until February 1937, a doctor would board each incoming ship to inspect the ship's documents and the health of passengers and crew to prevent serious infectious diseases from being introduced into New York by sea. On passenger vessels, the word of the captain concerning the health of his ship was generally accepted. Healthy ships received Pratique (see above).

Radio Pratique—An express form of Pratique established on 1 February 1937. Under this system, any ship inbound with a doctor aboard could radio in that the ship was in good health and request Pratique. The port medical office would then grant Pratique and the ship could proceed directly to her pier without the Quarantine stop. A ship on her maiden voyage to this country was an exception.

Raunt—An area of marshes and twisting channels in Jamaica Bay, north of the Beach Channel that runs along the inside of Rockaway Beach.

Red Hook Flats—An anchorage area above the Narrows, east of the main ship channel, along the Brooklyn shore, also referred to as Bay Ridge Flats.

Robbin's Reef—A rocky shoal in the Upper Bay off Staten Island, near the entrance to the Kill Van Kull. Originally named *Robbyns' Rift* by the Dutch after the harbor seals that frequented the rocks, it has been marked by a lighthouse since 1838.

Romer—A large shoal in Lower New York Bay, just southwest of the Ambrose Channel and east of the Swash Channel.

S.I.—Staten Island.

S.I. Lighthouse Depot—Formerly the Revenue Cutter Service base and yellow fever quarantine station in St. George, Staten Island. This small area next to the Staten Island Ferry Terminal became home to the United States Lighthouse Establishment Service. The depot was the main supply and repair center for the Fresnel lenses and brass lanterns and parts for U.S. lighthouses.

Scotland—A lightship stationed four miles west of Ambrose Channel light vessel, marking the approach to South Channel or Sandy Hook Channel.

Sea Anchor—An umbrella-like device trailed off the bow of a ship to keep her head to the wind and steady her movement during a storm.

Sheepshead Bay—Protected harbor and piers in southern Brooklyn, just west of the entrance to Jamaica Bay, and protected from open water by Rockaway Point. It is used mainly by charter fishing and dinner vessels smaller then 150 feet in overall length.

Spare Boy—In Sandy Hook Pilot terms, the entry-level position. The spare boy—usually a teenager—learned on the job, performing menial duties on board the pilot vessel for food but no pay, until he became proficient enough to be reliable.

Squat—The change of a ship's trim aft as it accelerates. As a ship develops more thrust, the stern sinks lower in the water.

Station—The ready position of pilot vessels outside New York Bay, also known as "Pilot Waters." Here, Sandy Hook Pilots board inbound vessels and depart outbound vessels. Today it is a triangular area, one corner being the sea buoy of Ambrose Channel, another the sea buoy of Sandy Hook Channel, and the last being Ambrose Light. The Outside Boat took station here.

Statue Anchorage—Now known as Liberty Anchorage, in the Upper Bay west of the Main Ship Channel and on the east side of Liberty Island.

Submarine Net—During wartime, a submarine net was suspended across the navigation channels to keep enemy submarines out of the port. During World War I a net was stretched across the Narrows between Staten Island and Brooklyn. During World War II, a net of steel cables was put into place between Hoffman Island and Norton Point, Coney Island, early in 1942. The net had a gate that could be opened to allow allied ships through.

Supercargo—A shipboard official normally in charge of the cargo.

Swash Channel—A shallow channel in the Lower Bay, just west of the Roamer Shoal, that cuts off the dogleg in the Main Ship Channel.

Swinburne Island, see Hoffman and Swinburne Islands.

Taffrail—Originally an ornamental rail along the upper edge of the stern.

Telegraph—Mechanical device used to signal desired engine speeds and directions from the officers in the wheelhouse (bridge) to the engine room and back.

Wallabout Bay—A deep bay on the Brooklyn side of the East River, above the Brooklyn Bridge. The Brooklyn Navy Yard fronted on Wallabout Bay.

Ward Line—The popular name for the New York & Cuba Mail Steamship Company, which provided regular service between New York and Southern ports, Cuba, and the West Indies.

Weehawken—A small town with Hudson River piers just across from 28th street, Manhattan.

West Bank—A shoal in the Lower Bay, south of Swinburne Island and just west of the Main Ship Channel. It is marked with a light.

Whistler—In general terms, a buoy fitted with a tube so air drawn in and compressed by the up-and-down movements of the waves is made to escape through a whistle and provide an audible position signal. Whistling buoys were introduced in the U.S. in 1876. Specifically, the Sandy Hook Pilots referred to the whistling buoy two and seven-eighths miles northwest by west 3/4 west of the Ambrose Channel light vessel, where the Ambrose Channel and Gedney Channel diverge, as the Whistler.

Yawl—Generally, a form of ship's boat, sometimes carried at the stern. Specifically, the boat used by the Sandy Hook Pilots to convey a pilot between the pilot vessel and a ship traveling within the port. Sandy Hook Pilot yawls were built by a number of boatbuilders in Staten Island and elsewhere. They were typically heavily built lapstrake boats about 18 feet long, with high sides, a full bow, and wide transom. Yawls were rowed by two apprentices, each pulling a 14-foot oar contained between heavy tholes on the gunwale.

Index

Index

Index